TFB

Δ

COTTON KNITTING

COTTON KNITTING

Over 30 Exclusive Patterns from Top Designers

Edited by Sally Harding

BARRON'S

Woodbury, New York • Toronto

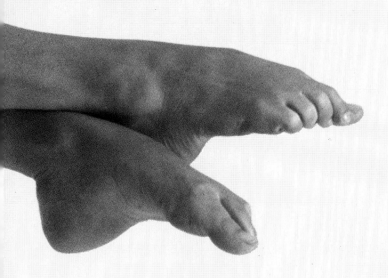

First U.S. edition published 1987 by Barron's Educational Series.

Text and illustrations © 1987 Frances Lincoln Limited.

Cotton Knitting was conceived, edited and produced by Frances Lincoln Limited, Apollo Works, 5 Charlton Kings Road, London NW5 2SB.

International Standard Book Number: 0-8120-5816-X
Library of Congress Catalog Card No. 86-26517
Library of Congress Cataloging in Publication Data
Cotton knitting.
1. Sweaters. 2. Knitting—Patterns. 3. Cotton yarn
I. Harding, Sally
TT825.C72   1987   746.9'2   86-26517
ISBN 0-8120-5816-X

PRINTED IN BELGIUM
789   987654321

CONTENTS

COLOR & COTTON	6
THE DESIGNS	
IN THE PINK	10
ORCHID SPRAY	14
NORDIC FAIR ISLE	18
ZIGZAG	21
ICE COOL	24
MONDRIAN SQUARES	26
FINESSE	30
BALLOONS	33
SPORTY STRIPES	36
CABLE CLASSIC	39
CABBAGE ROSE	42
SUGARED ALMOND	47
RACING COLORS	50
WAVEBAND	52
RAZZLE DAZZLE	56
CHECKERBOARD	59
FIESTA	62
RIPPLES	64
STRIPE SURPRISE	70
REGATTA	74
LACE UP	78
TIGER TAILS	80
SWEET CHESTNUT	86
CRAZY PAVING	88
BLOCKBUSTER	92
BASKETWEAVE	94
PRIMARY CABLES	96
COVER STORY	98
SUNSHINE	101
HOT SHOT	104
SNAKES & LADDERS	106
APPENDIX	
GAUGE & MEASUREMENTS	110
ABBREVIATIONS	111
BASIC TECHNIQUES	112
JOINING IN YARN	114
FINISHING	116
YARN MANUFACTURERS	119
ACKNOWLEDGMENTS	119
THE DESIGNERS	120

COLOR & COTTON

Cotton yarn is not uniformly graded in the same way that wool is. We have therefore divided the cotton yarns used by the designers in this book into four types. In the materials paragraph in the patterns, we specify fine, light and medium weights, and fancy yarns (bouclé, slub, chenille, terry, etc.). You will be able to match the correct yarn to the design with the help of the life-size yarn photograph found on the same page as the garment, and by checking yarn labels which usually recommend needle size and gauge. You *must* knit a gauge swatch to check the yarn before you start making the sweater (see page 110), changing the needles, if necessary, to give the specified gauge.

   Some of the designs are knitted using two strands of yarn throughout. Unless this is for the specific purpose of achieving subtle color effects (see page 33) or texture (see page 98), you could replace two strands of fine yarn, say, with one of a lightweight yarn but, again, the only way to check if this will measure the same as the pattern is to work a gauge swatch first.

The color scheme is a crucial factor in the success of any knitted garment. Many knitters follow the designer's color choice because it suits them or they lack the confidence to mix colors. To help you plan an alternative color scheme, we have shown knitted samples using alternative colors for some of the designs in this book. It is possible to mix colors successfully and to make quite radical and attractive changes to the original design as a result.

There are some simple guidelines to help you toward a successful choice. First, look at your main color choice and hold up at least four balls of the yarn to get some idea of the strength of the color when spread over a larger area. When you are mixing colors together, if the pattern is a large one, hold up a number of balls, but if it's a tiny pattern, hold strands of the yarn together to get a clearer idea of the final effect. Second, separate your choice of colors into the basic groups – the soft pastels, the striking bright colors, the neutrals and the strong but subtle shades – photographed below. Mix any of the colors in these groups with white and you will be successful, but mixing the first and last groups, for example, takes more skill. Good designers often break the "rules"

with great success (see Racing Colors, page 50), but you need a good color sense and a great deal of confidence in what looks good on you to succeed. If you are not sure of your choice, color in blocks with crayon or pencil to see how the colors work together to help you visualize the final effect.

The fashion drawings on these pages show how a designer has done this using two of the designs in the book. Mondrian Squares (see page 26), with its clear grid design, is easily worked in new colors. On one of the drawings, texture has been emphasized by the stitch patterns using a single neutral tone or shades of neutral tones. The bright version shows how different bright colors have been mixed together on a neutral background.

Crazy Paving (see page 88) is also designed around a frame of a single color. If you want to make a big statement, reverse the colors in the knitted sweater or fill in the frames with subtle shades or bright colors. The illustration on the left shows how similar tones – gray and pale yellow – take the boldness out of the design and give it a quiet, elegant sophistication. The sketched color squares show how much the design alters with different combinations.

The Mondrian Squares design is a classic shape that looks good with any number of different color combinations.

Crazy Paving is a more sophisticated pattern but offers a challenge when planning color variations.

Cotton yarns in different textures and finishes are grouped into pastels, brights, neutrals and subtle shades.

IN THE PINK

This polo-collared shirt can be knitted with long or short sleeves. You can choose from two other cable patterns, shown on page 13, to alter the effect.

■ SIZE
One size to fit up to 38" bust
See diagram for finished measurements.

■ MATERIALS
Use a medium weight cotton yarn.
29oz/800g for short sleeve version
32oz/900g for long sleeve version
One pair each of sizes 6 and 8 knitting needles *or size to obtain correct gauge*
One cable needle
Three ⅝" buttons

■ GAUGE
22 sts and 24 rows to 4" over St st using larger needles
To save time, take time to check gauge.

■ BACK
Using smaller needles, cast on 95 sts and work in rib as foll:
1st rib row (RS) K1, *P1, K1, rep from * to end.
2nd rib row P1, *K1, P1, rep from * to end.
Rep last 2 rows until ribbing measures 1¼", ending with a first row.
Inc row Rib 1, (M1, rib 3) 14 times, (M1, rib 2) 4 times, (M1, rib 3) 14 times, M1, rib 2. 128 sts.
Change to larger needles and work in pat as foll:
1st row (RS) P7, *K2, P3, K8, P3, K2, P3, K8, P3, K2*, P46, rep from * to *, P7.
2nd row K7, *P2, K3, P8, K3, P2, K3, P8, K3, P2*, K46, rep from * to *, K7.
3rd to 6th rows As first and 2nd.
7th row P7, *K2, P3, slip next 4 sts onto cable needle and hold at back of work, K4 from LH needle, K4 from cable needle – called C8 –, P3, K2, P3, C8, P3, K2*, P46, rep from * to *, P7.
8th row As 2nd row.
These 8 rows form pat.
Cont in pat without shaping until back measures 24" from beg, ending with a WS row.

Shoulder shaping
Bind off 11 sts at beg of next 8 rows.
Bind off rem 40 sts.

■ FRONT
Work as for back until front measures 11" from beg, ending with a RS row.
Divide for center front opening.
Next row (WS) Work 61 sts in pat, P1, (K1, P1) 3 times. Turn and leave rem sts on a spare needle.

Next row K1, (P1, K1) 3 times, work in pat to end.
Rep last 2 rows until opening measures 1¼", ending with a WS row.
Work buttonhole as foll:
1st buttonhole row Rib 3, bind off 2, rib 2, work in pat to end.
2nd buttonhole row Work in pat to last 7 sts, rib 2, cast on 2, rib 3.
Cont in pat and work another 2 buttonholes at 3" intervals.
Work 2 rows more in pat. (Front should now measure approx 19".)

Neck shaping
Next row With RS facing, bind off 16 sts, work in pat to end. 52 sts.
Work one row.
Keeping pat correct, dec one st at neck edge on next and every foll alternate row 7 times. 44 sts.
Work without shaping until front matches back to beg of shoulder shaping, ending with a RS row.

Shoulder shaping
Bind off 11 sts at beg of next and 2 foll alternate rows.
Work one row. Bind off rem 11 sts.
With WS facing, rejoin yarn to rem 60 sts, cast on 8 sts for button border. 68 sts.
Next row (WS) P1, (K1, P1) 3 times, work in pat to end.
Next row Work in pat to last 7 sts, K1, (P1, K1) 3 times.
Work to match first side, omitting buttonholes.

■ SLEEVES

**Using smaller needles, cast on 59 sts and work in rib as for back for 1¼", ending with a RS row.
Inc row Rib 1, (M1, rib 3) 8 times, (M1, rib 2) 4 times, (M1, rib 3) 8 times. M1, rib 2. 80 sts.**
Change to larger needles and work in pat as foll:
1st row (RS) K23, work from * to * as first row of back, P23.
2nd row P23, work from * to * as 2nd row of back, K23.
These 2 rows place center cable panel.
Shape sides by inc one st at each end of every 3rd row until there are 100 sts.
Cont without shaping until sleeve measures 11" from beg.
Bind off.

■ COLLAR

Join shoulder seams.
With RS facing and using smaller needles, beg in middle of right front band and pick up and K40 sts up right front neck, 35 sts across back neck and 40 sts down left front neck to center of left front band. 115 sts.
Work in rib as for back for 4", beg with a 2nd row.
Bind off loosely in rib.

■ FINISHING

Sew sleeve edge to front and back, placing center of cable panel at shoulder seam.
Join side and sleeve seams.
Sew cast-on edge of left front band underneath right front band.
Sew on buttons.
Press seams only.

LONG SLEEVE VERSION

■ BACK AND FRONT

Work as for short sleeve version.

■ SLEEVES

Work as for short sleeve version from ** to **.
Change to larger needles and work in pat as for short sleeve version, **and at the same time** shape sides by inc one st at each end of every 7th row until there are 100 sts.
Work without shaping until sleeve measures 17½" from beg. Bind off.

■ FINISHING AND COLLAR

Work as for short sleeve version.

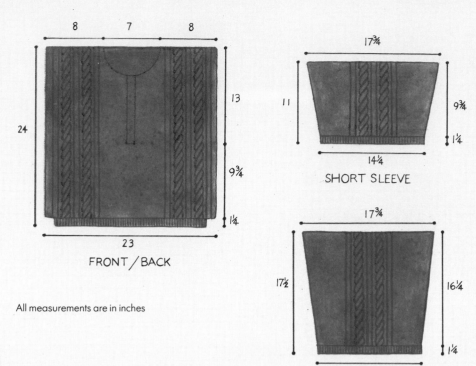

FRONT / BACK

All measurements are in inches

SHORT SLEEVE

LONG SLEEVE

These four samples show the three cable stitches knitted in alternative bright colors.

CABLE VARIATIONS

You may like to vary the design by knitting this classic shirt shape with a different cable pattern. Remember to check your gauge before embarking on the new pattern. The two cables shown in the red and blue variations below can be incorporated into the master pattern by using the pattern below to replace the stitches that appear between the * and * in the main pattern.

RED CABLE

1st row K2, P3,(sl 2 sts onto cable needle, hold at back of work, K2, then K2 from cable needle – called CB4 –,) twice, P3, K2, P3, CB4 twice, P3, K2.
2nd row P2, K3, P8, K3, P2, K3, P8, K3, P2.

3rd row K2, P3, (sl 2 sts onto cable needle, hold at front of work, K2, then K2 from cable needle – called CF4 –,) twice, P3, K2, P3, CF4 twice, P3, K2.
4th row As 2nd row.
These 4 rows form pat.

BLUE CABLE

1st row K2, P4, K2, P2, K2, P4, K2, P4, K2, P2, K2, P4, K2.
2nd row P2, K4, P2, K2, P2, K4, P2, K4, P2, K2, P2, K4, P2.
3rd row K2, P4, sl next 4 sts onto cable needle and hold at front of work, K2, sl 2 purl sts from cable needle back onto LH needle, pass the cable needle to back of work, P2 from LH needle, K2 from cable needle – called MB4 –, P4, K2, P4, MB4, P4, K2.
4th row and every alternate row As 2nd row.
5th row and every alternate row As first row.
10th row As 2nd row.
These 10 rows form pat.

ORCHID SPRAY

This cardigan can easily be converted to a vest by leaving off the sleeves and making armhole bands. For a simple design, leave out the orchid motif.

SIZE

To fit 32-34[36:38-40]" bust
Figures for larger sizes are in brackets. Where there is only one set of figures, this applies to all sizes.
See diagram for finished measurements.

MATERIALS

Use a fine cotton fleck yarn and a viscose yarn knitted together throughout for the main color (A). Use a lightweight cotton yarn for contrasting colors.
17[17:18]oz/475[475:500]g main color A viscose (silver)
10[11:12]oz/275[300:325]g main color A cotton (beige/pink fleck)
1oz/30g first contrast B (pink)
2oz/40g 2nd contrast C (green)
1oz/25g 3rd contrast D (yellow)
1oz/30g 4th contrast E (blue)
For vest version:
12[12:13]oz/325[325:350]g main color A viscose
8[8:9]oz/225[225:250]g main color A cotton
One pair each of sizes 7 and 9 knitting needles *or size to obtain correct gauge.*
One size B crochet hook
One pair shoulder pads
Two 1¼" buttons, three ¾" buttons
Bobbins

GAUGE

16 sts and 20 rows to 4" over St st using larger needles
To save time, take time to check gauge.

Note

Read chart from right to left for RS knit rows and left to right for WS purl rows. Unless stated St st is used throughout. Do not carry colors across; use a separate bobbin of yarn for each color section. When changing colors, pick up new color from under dropped color to prevent holes (see page 114).

BACK

Using smaller needles and A, cast on 83[89:95] sts and work in rib as foll:
1st rib row (RS) K1, *P1, K1, rep from * to end.
2nd rib row P1, *K1, P1, rep from * to end.
Rep last 2 rows until rib measures 1¼", ending with a 2nd rib row and inc one st in last row. 84[90:96] sts.
Change to larger needles and work without shaping from row 1 of chart for back (outer line) to the end of row 62.

Armhole shaping

Bind off 6 sts at beg of next 2 rows. Dec one st at each end of next and every alternate row 4 times in all. 64[70:76] sts.
Cont without shaping to the end of row 116.

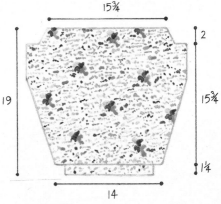

SLEEVE

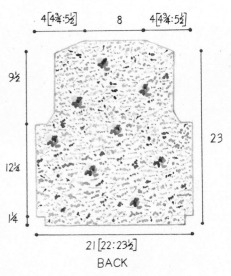

BACK

RIGHT FRONT

All measurements are in inches

Shoulder shaping

Bind off 5[6:7] sts at beg of next 4 rows.
Bind off 6[7:8] sts at beg of next 2 rows.
Bind off rem 32 sts.

RIGHT FRONT

Using larger needles and A, cast on 2 sts, and work from row 1 of chart for front as foll:
1st row Work in pat to end.
2nd row Inc one st at beg of row, work in pat to end.
3rd row Inc one st at each end of row.
4th row Cast on 3 sts at beg of row, work in pat to last st, inc one st.
Rep last 2 rows 5 times. (14th row of chart) 39 sts.
Next row Inc one st at beg of row, work in pat to last 0[1:1] st, inc 0[1:1].
Next row Cast on 0[2:3] sts, work in pat to last st, inc one st.
Next row Inc one st at beg of row, work in pat to last 0[0:0] st, inc one st.
Next row Inc 0[0:1] st, work in pat to end. 42[45:48] sts.
Cont without shaping to the end of row 56 of chart.

Front shaping

Next row (RS) Dec one st at beg of row, work in pat to end.
Work in pat for 4 rows without shaping.
Rep last 5 rows to end of row 79 of chart. 37[40:43] sts.

Armhole shaping

Next row (WS) Bind off 4[5:6] sts, work in pat to end.
Work one row.
Cont to dec at front edge on every 5th row from previous dec, **and at the same time** dec one st at armhole edge on next and every alternate row 3 times more. 27[29:31] sts.
Keeping armhole edge straight, cont to dec at front edge on every 5th row from previous dec to the end of row 133. 18:[20:22] sts.

Shoulder shaping

Bind off 5[6:7] sts at beg of next and 2 foll alternate rows.
Bind off rem 8 sts.

LEFT FRONT

Work as for right front, reversing all shapings and working a mirror image of chart by beg with a P row instead of a K row.

SLEEVES

Using smaller needles and A, cast on 43 sts and work in rib as for back for 1¼", ending with a WS row.
Inc row Rib 4, (M1, rib 3) 13 times. 56 sts.
Change to larger needles and work from sleeve chart (thicker line on back chart) as foll:

Inc one st at each end of 3rd and every foll 4th row to 84 sts.
Cont without shaping until the end of row 80.

Cap shaping
Bind off 6 sts at beg of next 2 rows.
Dec one st at each end of next and every foll alternate row 4 times in all. 64 sts.
Bind off.

■ BACK BELT
Using smaller needles and A, cast on 13 sts and work in K1, P1 rib for 8".
Bind off loosely in rib.

■ FINISHING
**To finish pointed edges on fronts, crochet a single crochet edging along pointed edges to give a straighter edge.
Work each side of point separately.
Darn in all ends. Following manufacturer's directions, block pieces to finished measurements (see page 118).**
Join shoulder seams.
Sew top of sleeve to armhole edge.
Join sleeve and side seams.

■ FRONT BAND
With RS facing and using smaller needles and A, pick up and K109 sts evenly up right front edge to center back neck and 110 sts down left front edge. 219 sts.
Work in P1, K1 rib for one row.
1st buttonhole row Rib 3, bind off 3, (rib 12, bind off 3) twice, rib 183.
2nd buttonhole row Rib 183, cast on 3, (rib 12, cast on 3) twice, rib 3.
Work 2 rows more in rib.
Bind off loosely in rib.
Sew smaller buttons to front band.
Attach belt by sewing one large button at each end, placing belt at waist level approx 4" from lower edge at center back of garment.

VEST VERSION

■ BACK AND FRONTS
Work as for cardigan.

■ ARMHOLE BANDS
Join shoulder seams.
With RS facing and using smaller needles and A, pick up and K96 sts around armhole.
Work in K1, P1 rib for 1¼".
Bind off loosely in rib.

■ FINISHING
Work as for cardigan version from ** to **.
Join side and armhole band seam.
Work front band and complete as for cardigan.

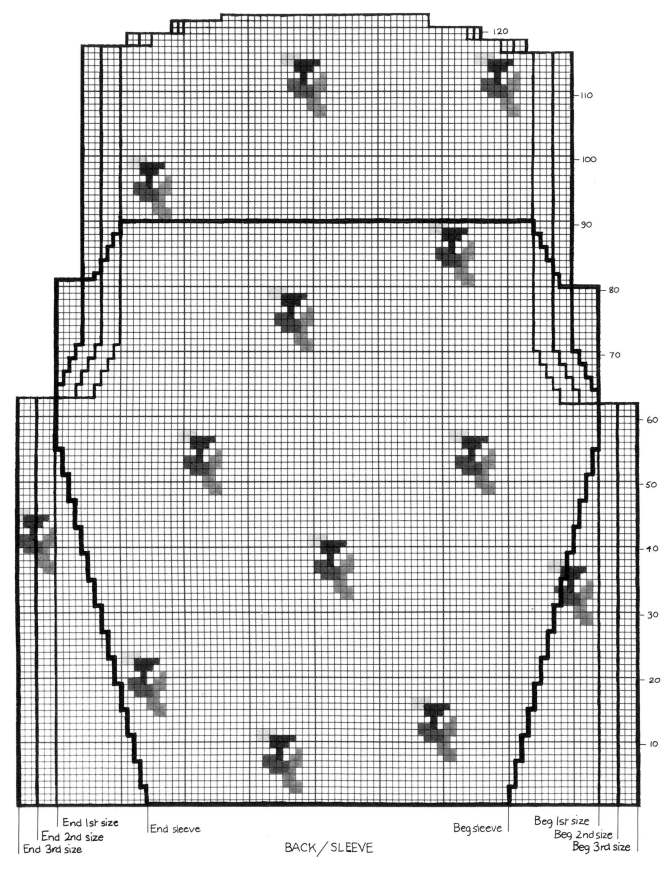

120

110

100

90

80

70

60

50

40

30

20

10

End 1st size

End 2nd size

End 3rd size

End sleeve

Beg sleeve

Beg 1st size

Beg 2nd size

Beg 3rd size

BACK / SLEEVE

130

120

110

100

90

80

70

60

50

40

30

20

10

End 1st size
End 2nd size
End 3rd size

All sizes

RIGHT FRONT

130

120

110

100

90

80

70

60

50

40

30

20

10

End 1st size
End 2nd size
End 3rd size

All sizes

ALTERNATIVE FRONT

17

NORDIC FAIR ISLE

A favorite in any yarn, this black and gold Fair Isle sleeveless sweater has a black plain knitted back.

■ SIZE

To fit 32[34:36]" bust
Figures for larger sizes are given in brackets. Where there is only one set of figures, this applies to all sizes.
See diagram for finished measurements.

■ MATERIALS

Use a fine mercerized cotton yarn.
8[9:10]oz/200[225:250]g main color A (black)
2[2:3]oz/50[50:75]g first contrast B (sand)
2[2:3]oz/50[50:75]g 2nd contrast C (beige)
2[2:3]oz/50[50:75]g 3rd contrast D (gray)
One pair each of sizes 2 and 4 knitting needles *or size to obtain correct gauge*

■ GAUGE

32 sts and 36 rows to 4" over Fair Isle pat using larger needles
31 sts and 36 rows to 4" over St st using larger needles
To save time, take time to check gauge.

Note

Read chart from right to left for RS knit rows and left to right for WS purl rows. Carry colors not in use loosely across wrong side of work, weaving yarn in on every 2nd st where appropriate (see page 115). Cut and join colors as required.

■ FRONT

Using smaller needles and A, cast on 133[139:145] sts and work in rib as foll:
**1st rib row (RS) K1, *P1, K1, rep from * to end.
2nd rib row P1, *K1, P1, rep from * to end.
Rep last 2 rows until rib measures 2", ending with a first row.**
Inc row P22[13:9] (M1, P44[28:21]) 2[4:6] times, M1, P23[14:10].
136[144:152] sts.
Change to larger needles and work without shaping in Fair Isle pat from row 1 of chart until front measures 13¾[14½:15¼]", ending with a WS row.

Armhole shaping

Keeping pat correct, bind off 12 sts at beg of next 2 rows. 112[120:128] sts.
Dec one st at each end of next 2 rows. 108[116:124] sts.

Neck shaping

Next row Keeping pat correct, pat 54[58:62] sts, turn and leave rem sts on a spare needle.
Dec one st at armhole edge on next and every foll alternate row, **and at the same time** dec one st at neck edge on next and every foll 3rd row until 8[10:12] dec have been worked at armhole edge.
Keeping armhole edge straight cont neck shaping only until 22[24:26] sts rem.
Cont in pat without shaping until front measures 24[24¾:26]".
Bind off.
Rejoin yarn to rem 54[58:62] sts and complete to match first side, reversing shapings.

■ BACK

Using smaller needles and A, cast on 131[137:143] sts and work in rib as for front from ** to **.
Next row P, inc one st at center of row. 132[138:144] sts.
Change to larger needles and beg with a K row, work in St st using A only until back measures same as front to armhole.

Armhole shaping

Bind off 10 sts at beg of next 2 rows. 112[118:124] sts.
Dec one st at each end of next 2 rows. 108[114:120] sts.
Dec one st at each end of next and every alternate row until 92[96:100] sts rem.
Cont without shaping until back measures 1¼" less than front to shoulder, ending with a WS row.

Neck shaping

Next row (RS) K27[29:31] sts, turn and leave rem sts on a spare needle.
Dec one st at neck edge on next 5 rows. 22[24:26] sts.
Work without shaping until back measures same as front to shoulder.
Bind off.
With RS facing, rejoin yarn to rem sts, bind off center 38 sts and work to match first side, reversing shaping.

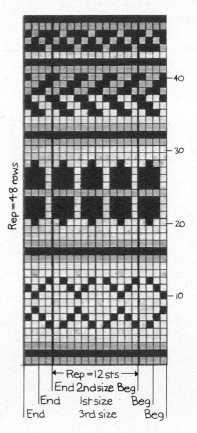

Rep = 48 rows

40

30

20

10

←Rep = 12 sts→
End 2nd size Beg
End   Beg
1st size
End   Beg
3rd size

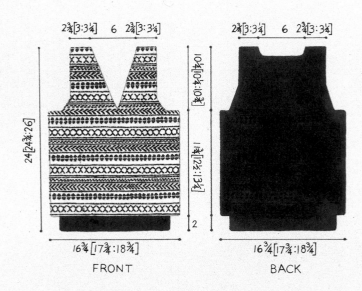

2¾[3:3¼] 6 2¾[3:3¼]

10¼[10¼:10¾]

11¾[12¼:13¾]

2

24[24¾:26]

16¾[17¾:18¾]

FRONT

2¾[3:3¼] 6 2¾[3:3¼]

16¾[17¾:18¾]

BACK

All measurements are in inches

NECKBAND

Join right shoulder.
With RS facing, using smaller needles and A, pick up and K81[84:86] sts down left front neck, one st from center front (mark this st), 81[84:86] sts up right front neck, 6 sts down right back neck, 38 sts across back neck, 6 sts up left back neck. 213[219:223] sts.
Work in P1, K1 rib for 6 rows, dec one st at each side of center st on every row.

Bind off evenly in rib. Join left shoulder and neckband.

ARMHOLE BORDERS

With RS facing, using smaller needles and A, pick up and K171[179:187] sts evenly around armhole.
Work in P1, K1, rib for 6 rows.
Bind off evenly in rib.

FINISHING

Following manufacturer's directions, block pieces to finished measurements (see page 118).
Join side and armhole border seams.

These alternative color schemes for the sleeveless sweater on the preceding page all have a dominant theme of red, yet look very different, demonstrating how flexible Fair Isle patterns are. Choose one dominant color or perhaps two and then select the contrasts carefully.

ZIGZAG

The special design touches – the bell ruffle at the neck and shoulders and the multicolored rib – add a touch of class to a relatively plain shape. The ruffle on the shoulders forms part of the sleeves, which are knitted directly onto the body of the sweater.

■ SIZE

One size to fit up to 38" bust
See diagram for finished measurements.

■ MATERIALS

Use a lightweight cotton yarn.
15oz/400g main color A (slate)
4oz/100g contrast B (rust)
2oz/50g contrast C (pink)
2oz/50g contrast D (gold)
2oz/50g contrast E (light gray)
4oz/100g contrast F (beige)
2oz/50g contrast G (heather)
One each of 24" long sizes 3 and 5 circular knitting needles *or size to obtain correct gauge*

■ GAUGE

24 sts and 30 rows to 4" over St st using larger needle
To save time, take time to check gauge.

Note

Body of garment is worked in one piece to armholes.

■ WAISTBAND

Knitted as a strip in "ridge and furrow" pat.
Using smaller needle and B, cast on 24 sts, and work in pat as foll:

1st row Using B, K.
2nd row Using B, P.
3rd row Change to A, K.
4th row Using A, K.
5th row Using A, P.
6th row Using A, K.
7th row As first row using next color in sequence (E).
Rows 2-7 form pat. A is used for all "ridges" (rows 3-6) and colors for "furrows" are used in sequence of B,E,C,D,G,F. Cont until band measures 31" slightly stretched, ending with a "ridge".
Bind off and sew up to make a band.

■ BODY

Using larger circular needle and C, pick up and K264 sts around the more uneven edge of waistband.
Purl one round using C.
Cont without shaping, working from row 1 of body chart and using colors as indicated on color chart, until body measures 4" from beg of pat.

Divide for back

Next row Pat 132 sts, turn and leave rem sts on a spare needle.
Work one row.

Armhole shaping

Bind off 14 sts at beg of next 2 rows. 104 sts.
Cont in pat as set, working back and forth until armhole measures approx 12", ending with a "ridge". Leave sts on a spare needle.

■ FRONT

Rejoin yarn to rem sts and work as for back until armhole measures 9", ending with a WS row.

Neck shaping

Next row Patt 37 sts, turn and leave rem sts on a spare needle.
Dec one st at neck edge on every row until 27 sts rem.
Cont without shaping until front measures same as back to shoulder.
Leave sts on a spare needle.
With RS facing, slip center 30 sts onto a holder, rejoin yarn to rem sts and work to match first side, reversing shaping.

Join shoulders

Place 27 sts of front parallel with 27 sts of corresponding back shoulder with WS together and using a smaller needle and C, bind off and work picot ridge as foll:
Knit through back and front and bind

Worked in st st except for ridge rows. When working in the round, ridges are worked as K one round, P one round. When working back and forth in rows, ridges are worked as K2 rows.

PATTERN CHART

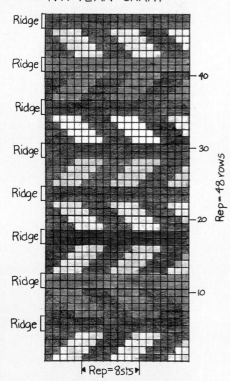

Ridge
Ridge
Ridge — 40
Ridge — 30
Ridge
Ridge — 20
Ridge
Ridge — 10
Ridge

Rep = 48 rows

|◄ Rep=8 sts ►|

SLEEVE SHAPING

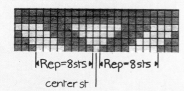

|◄ Rep=8 sts ►|◄ Rep=8 sts ►|
center st

When working sleeve, slant diagonals in opposite directions on each side of center st.
Keep pat correct on each side of center st when decreasing.

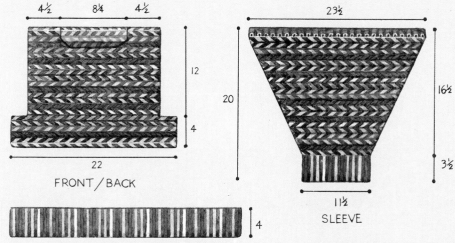

FRONT / BACK
4½ 8¼ 4½
12
4
22

RIB
31
4

SLEEVE
23½
16½
3½
11½

All measurements are in inches

off 3 sts, *put st on RH needle back onto the front of LH needle, cast on 2 sts, K and bind off 3 sts, rep from * until all sts are bound off. Leave center 50 sts on a holder for back neck and work other shoulder, beg at side edge.

2nd row *K5, P3, rep from * to last 6 sts, K6.
3rd row P6, *yo, K3, yo, P5, rep from * to end.
4th row *K5, P5, rep from * to last 6 sts, K6.
5th row P6, *yo, K5, yo, P5, rep from * to end.
6th row *K5, P7, rep from * to last 6 sts, K6.
7th row P6, *yo, K7, yo, P5, rep from * to end.
8th row *K5, P9, rep from * to last 6 sts K6.
9th row Change to E, P6, *bind off the 8 sts of the "bell", P5, rep from * to end. 144 sts.

NECKBAND

With RS facing and using smaller circular needle and E, K50 sts from back neck, pick up and K17 sts down left side of neck, K30 sts from front neck and pick up and K17 sts up right side of neck. 114 sts.
Make ruffle as foll:
1st round P3, *cast on 8 sts onto RH needle, P6, rep from * to last 3 sts, cast on 8, P3.
2nd round Change to A, P3, *K8, P6, rep from * to last 11 sts, K8, P3.
3rd round As 2nd round.
4th round P3, *sl 1, K1, psso, K4, K2tog, P6, rep from * to last 11 sts, sl 1, K1, psso, K4, K2tog, P3.
5th round P3, *K6, P6, rep from * to last 9 sts, K6, P3.
6th round P3, *sl 1, K1, psso, K2, K2tog, P6, rep from * to last 9 sts, sl 1, K1, psso, K2, K2tog, P3.

10th row K, cast on one st. 145 sts. Change to larger needle and work in pat from row 1 of sleeve chart, reversing order of colors and dec each side of center st on 3rd and every foll 4th row as foll:
3rd row Pat 70 sts, sl 1, K1, psso, K1 (center st), K2tog, pat rem 70 sts.
7th row Pat 69 sts, sl 1, K1, psso, K1 (center st), K2tog, pat rem 69 sts.
Cont dec as set until sleeve measures approx 16½" from "ridge" in color C at beg, ending with a complete pat.
Next row Using C, K, dec evenly to 56 sts. Bind off in C.

CUFFS

With RS facing and using smaller needle and B, cast on 20 sts and work as for waistband until 15 ridges are completed.
Bind off on 4th row of 15th ridge.

7th round P3, *K4, P6, rep from * to last 7 sts, K4, P3.
8th round P3, *sl 1, K1, psso, K2tog, P6, rep from * to last 7 sts, sl 1, K1, psso, K2tog, P3.
9th round P3, *K2, P6, rep from * to last 5 sts, K2, P3.
10th round P3, *K2tog, P6, rep from * to last 5 sts, K2tog, P3.
11th round P3, *K1, P6, rep from * to last 4 sts, K1, P3.
12th round P3, *K2tog, P5, rep from * to last 4 sts, K2tog, P2. 114 sts.
13th round Using C, K. Bind off.

FINISHING

Sew cuffs to lower edge of sleeve, stretching to fit. Sew sleeve to bound-off sts at underarm and join sleeve seam.
Following manufacturer's directions, block sweater to finished measurements (see page 118).

SLEEVES

With RS facing and using larger needle and C, pick up and K144 sts evenly around armhole.
Knit one row.
Change to smaller needle and A, knit one row.
Next row *K5, P1, rep from * to end.
Work bell ruffle as foll:
1st row (RS) P6, *yo, K1, yo, P5, rep from * to end.

ICE COOL

Fine lightweight cotton and a flattering shoulder line make this a perfect summer top. A variation of the same cable pattern can be adapted to a boat neck top.

■ SIZE

One size to fit up to 38" bust
See diagram for finished measurements.

■ MATERIALS

9oz/250g fine cotton yarn for round neck version
15oz/400g fine cotton novelty yarn for boat neck version
One pair each of sizes 2 and 3 knitting needles *or size to obtain correct gauge*
One cable needle

■ GAUGE

16 sts and 16 rows to 4" over St st using larger needles
To save time, take time to check gauge.

■ BACK

**Using smaller needles, cast on 119 sts and work in rib as foll:
1st rib row (RS) K1, *P1, K1, rep from * to end.
2nd rib row P1, *K1, P1, rep from * to end.
Rep last 2 rows until rib measures 2", ending with a 2nd rib row and inc one st in last row. 120 sts.
Change to larger needles and work in pat as foll:
1st row K1, slip first st onto cable needle and leave at front of work, K1, then K1 from cable needle, – called T2 –, (K winding yarn around needle twice – called KW) 24 times, (K6, KW24) 3 times, T2, K1.
2nd and every alternate row P3, K24, (P6, K24) 3 times, P3.

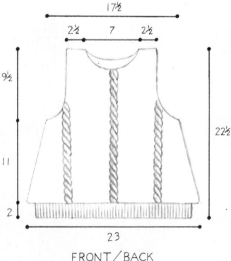

FRONT/BACK

All measurements are in inches

3rd row As first row.
5th row K1, T2, KW24, slip next 3 sts onto cable needle and leave at front of work, K3, then K3 from cable needle – called C6 –, (KW24, C6) twice, KW24, T2, K1.
7th row As first row.
8th row As 2nd row.
**Cont in pat as set, and at the same time keeping 3 edge sts correct, dec one st at each end of next and every foll 7th row (3 sts in) until 92 sts rem (keeping cable panels correct). Cont without shaping until back measures 13", ending with a WS row.

Armhole shaping
Bind off 5 sts at beg of next 2 rows.
Keeping 3 edge sts correct, dec one st (3 sts in) at each end of next and every foll 3rd row until 60 sts rem.
Cont without shaping until back measures 20½".

Back neck shaping
Pat 19 sts, turn and leave rem sts on a spare needle.
Next row P3, K to last 3 sts, P3.
Keeping 3 edge sts correct, dec one st at neck edge (3 sts in) on next and 5 foll alternate rows.
Work one row.
Bind off rem 13 sts.
With RS facing, rejoin yarn to rem sts, bind off center 22 sts and work to match first side, reversing all shaping.

■ **FRONT**
Work as for back until front measures 19".

Front neck shaping
Next row Pat 21 sts, turn and leave rem sts on a spare needle.
Next row P3, K to last 3 sts, P3.
Keeping 3 edge sts correct dec one st at neck edge (3 sts in) on next and 7 foll alternate rows. 13 sts.
Work a few rows without shaping until front measures same as back to shoulder.
Bind off.
With RS facing, rejoin yarn to rem sts, bind off center 18 sts and work to match first side, reversing all shaping.

■ **NECKBAND**
Join right shoulder seam.
With RS facing and using smaller needles, pick up and K25 sts down left front, K18 sts across center front, K25 sts up right front, K16 sts down right back neck, K22 across center back and K15 sts up left back neck. 121 sts.
Work in rib as for back for 5 rows.
Bind off loosely in rib.

■ **ARMHOLE BANDS**
Join left shoulder and neckband seam.

With RS facing and using smaller needles, pick up and K111 sts evenly around armhole.
Work in rib as back for 5 rows.
Bind off loosely in rib.

■ **FINISHING**
Join side and armband seams.

BOAT NECK TOP

■ **BACK AND FRONT** (alike)
Work as for back of round neck version from ** to **.
Keeping the 3 edge sts correct, cont in pat as set until work measures 13", ending with a WS row.

Armhole shaping
Bind off 5 sts at beg of next 2 rows. 110 sts.
Keeping 3 edge sts correct, cont without shaping until work measures 22".
Bind off.

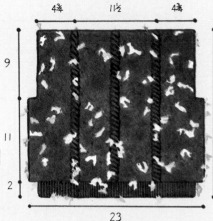

FRONT / BACK

All measurements are in inches

■ **FINISHING**
Join shoulders for 4¾".
Join side seams.

MONDRIAN SQUARES

A simple shape provides the "canvas" for these Mondrian-style blocks of color. The neat shirt collar and classic shape would suit any member of the family. Try alternative color schemes — vibrant, cool or autumnal — to suit different personalities.

■ SIZE
To fit 32-34 [36-38]" bust
Figures for larger sizes are given in brackets. Where there is only one set of figures, this applies to all sizes. *See diagram for finished measurements.*

■ MATERIALS
Use a lightweight cotton yarn.
22[23]oz/620[650]g main color A (white)
2[2]oz/30[40]g first contrast B (black)
4[5]oz/100[120]g 2nd contrast C (yellow)
One pair each of sizes 4 and 6 knitting needles *or size to obtain correct gauge*

■ GAUGE
17 sts and 25 rows to 4" over seed st using larger needles
To save time, take time to check gauge.

Note
Read chart from right to left for RS odd-numbered rows and left to right for even-numbered rows.
Do not carry colors across; use a separate bobbin of color for each color section. When changing colors, pick up new color from under dropped color to prevent holes (see page 114).

■ STITCHES
Seed st (Main color A only)
Worked over even number of sts.
1st row *K1, P1, rep from * to end.
2nd row *P1, K1, rep from * to end.
These 2 rows form pat.
Worked over odd number of sts.
1st row K1, *P1, K1, rep from * to end.
This row forms pat.

Stockinette st (B and C only)
1st row (RS) K.
2nd row P.
These 2 rows form pat.

■ BACK
Using smaller needles, cast on 81[93] sts as foll:
20[26]A, 1B, 19A, 1B, 19A, 1B, 20[26]A.
Keeping to colors as set, work in rib as foll:
1st rib row K1, *P1, K1, rep from * to end.
2nd rib row P1, *K1, P1, rep from * to end.

Rep last 2 rows until rib measures 3¼", ending with a first row.
First size only:
Inc row Rib 5, (M1 , rib 5) 3 times, [rib 4, (M1, rib 4) 4 times] twice, rib 6 (M1, rib 5) 3 times. 95 sts.
2nd size only:
Inc row (Rib 5, M1) 5 times, rib 5, (M1, rib 4) 4 times, (rib 4, M1) 4 times, (rib 6, M1) 4 times, rib 7. 110 sts.
Both sizes:
Change to larger needles and work without shaping in pats from chart, making sure color B continues in correct position.
Place marker at each end of row 65[79] for armholes.
When chart is complete bind off.

■ FRONT
Work as for back to end of row 120[134].

Neck shaping
Next row Pat 42[49] sts, turn and leave rem sts on a spare needle. Bind off 2 sts at neck edge on next 5 rows. 32[39] sts.
Cont without shaping until front matches back to shoulder.
Bind off.
Rejoin yarn to rem sts, bind off center 11[12] sts and work to match first side, reversing shaping.

■ SLEEVES
Using larger needles, cast on 38 sts as foll:
19A, 1B, 18A.
Work in pat of A in seed st and B in St st without shaping for 36 rows.
Now work from chart, shaping sides by inc one st at each end of 4th and every foll 3rd row until there are 96 sts.
Cont without shaping for 12 rows to end of sleeve chart.
Bind off.

■ COLLAR

Using larger needles and A, cast on 14 sts and work in seed st for 128 rows. Bind off.

■ FINISHING

Following manufacturer's directions, block pieces to finished measurements (see page 118).
Join shoulder seams.
Sew bound-off edge of sleeves to back and front between markers.
Join side and sleeve seams.
Sew row ends of collar to neck edge.

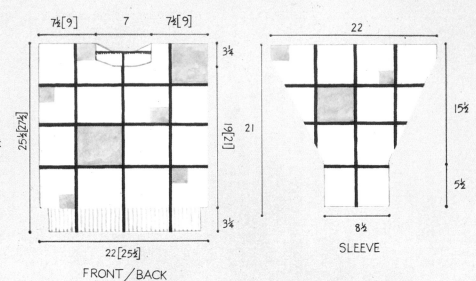

FRONT / BACK

All measurements are in inches

SLEEVE

This shape and design can easily be altered to change its appeal and personality. It works well no matter which way you use the colors: it is equally effective if you reverse the black, neutral and brown or use three strong colors together, such as purple, black and pink.

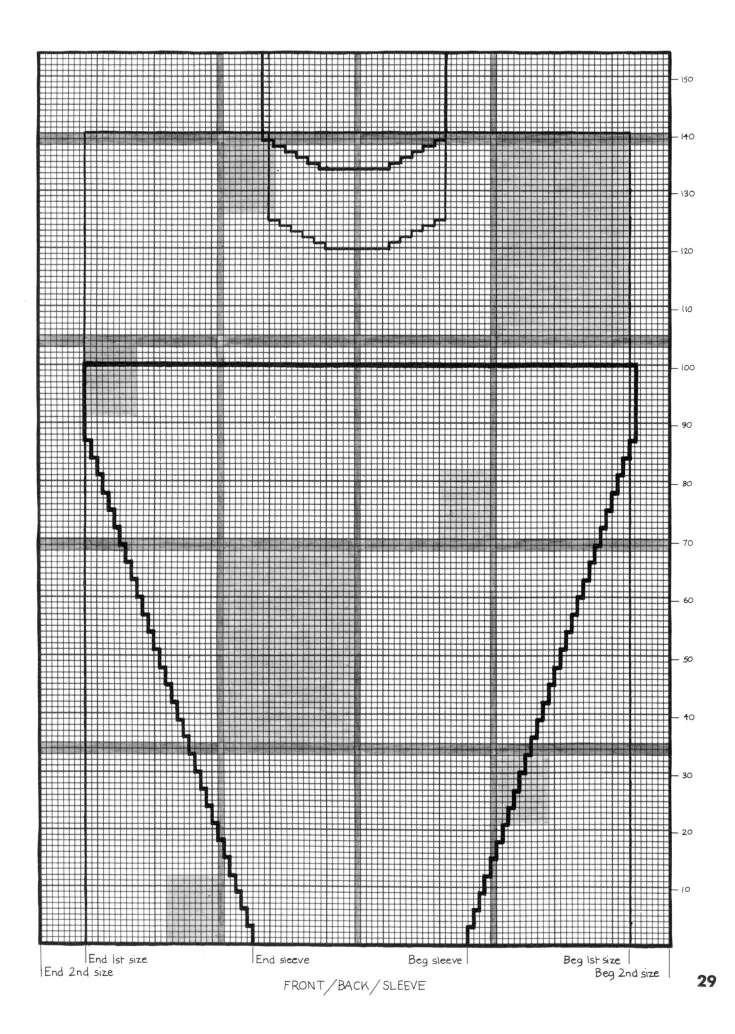

End 2nd size | End 1st size | End sleeve | Beg sleeve | Beg 1st size | Beg 2nd size

FRONT / BACK / SLEEVE

29

FINESSE

This beautifully crafted long-line classic has a lace pattern knitted within a twisted stitch panel on the body and the sleeves. A smaller lace pattern is provided on page 32 for the panels.

■ SIZE

To fit 32-34[36:38:40]" bust
Figures for larger sizes are given in brackets. Where there is only one set of figures, this applies to all sizes. *See diagram for finished measurements.*

■ MATERIALS

20[22:23]oz/550[600:650]g fine mercerized cotton yarn
One pair each of sizes 2 and 4 knitting needles *or size to obtain correct gauge*
One cable needle

■ GAUGE

28 sts and 40 rows to 4" over pat st using larger needles
To save time, take time to check gauge.

■ BACK

Using smaller needles, cast on 110[114:118] sts and work in rib as foll:
1st rib row (RS) K2, *P2, K2, rep from * to end.
2nd rib row P2, *K2, P2, rep from * to end.
Rep last 2 rows until ribbing measures 6", ending with a WS row.
Inc row Rib 3, (M1, rib 4) 10[6:2] times, (M1, rib 3) 9[21:33] times, (M1, rib 4) 10[6:2] times. 139[147:155] sts.
Change to larger needles and work in pat as foll:
Note See "lace panel variation" on page 32 for altering cable between † and †.
1st row K13[17:21], (P1, K11) 3 times, P1, K1 tbl, P1, slip next 3 sts onto cable needle, turn cable needle and knit 3rd, 2nd and first st – called T3 –, P1, K1 tbl, P1, †K11, yo, K2tog, K10, †P1, K1 tbl, P1, T3, P1, K1 tbl, P1, (K11, P1) 3 times, K13[17:21].
2nd row and every alternate row P.
3rd row K13[17:21], (P1, K11) 3 times, P1, K1 tbl, P1, K3, P1, K1 tbl, P1, †K9, K2tog, yo, K1, yo, sl 1, K1, psso, K9, †P1, K1 tbl, P1, K3, P1, K1 tbl, P1, (K11, P1) 3 times, K13[17:21].
5th row K13[17:21], (P1, K11) 3 times, P1, K1 tbl, P1, T3, P1, K1 tbl, P1, †K8, K2tog, yo, K3, yo, sl 1, K1, psso, K8, †P1, K1 tbl, P1, T3, P1, K1 tbl, P1, (K11, P1) 3 times, K13[17:21].
7th row K13[17:21], (P1, K11) 3 times, P1, K1 tbl, P1, K3, P1, K1 tbl, P1, †K7, K2tog, yo, K5, yo, sl 1, K1, psso, K7,

†P1, K1 tbl, P1, K3, P1, K1 tbl, P1, (K11, P1) 3 times, K13[17:21].
9th row K13[17:21], (P1, K11) 3 times, P1, K1 tbl, P1, T3, P1, K1 tbl, P1, †K6 K2tog, yo, K7, yo, sl 1, K1, psso, K6, †P1, K1 tbl, P1, T3, P1, K1 tbl, P1, (K11, P1) 3 times, K13[17:21].
11th row K13[17:21], (P1, K11) 3 times, P1, K1 tbl, P1, K3, P1, K1 tbl, P1, K5, K2tog, yo, K9, yo, sl 1, K1, psso, K5, †P1, K1 tbl, P1, K3, P1, K1 tbl, P1, (K11, P1) 3 times, K13[17:21].
13th row K13[17:21], (P1, K11) 3 times, P1, K1 tbl, P1, T3, P1, K1 tbl, P1, †K4, K2tog, yo, K11, yo, sl 1, K1, psso, K4, †P1, K1 tbl, P1, T3, P1, K1 tbl, P1, (K11, P1) 3 times, K13[17:21].
15th row K13[17:21], (P1, K11) 3 times, P1, K1 tbl, P1, K3, P1, K1 tbl, P1, †K3, K2tog, yo, K13, yo, sl 1, K1, psso, K3, †P1, K1 tbl, P1, K3, P1, K1 tbl, P1, (K11, P1) 3 times, K13[17:21].
17th row K13[17:21], (P1, K11) 3 times, P1, K1 tbl, P1, T3, P1, K1 tbl, P1, †K2, K2tog, yo, K15, yo, sl 1, K1, psso, K2, †P1, K1 tbl, P1, T3, P1, K1 tbl, P1, (K11, P1) 3 times, K13[17:21].
19th row K13[17:21], (P1, K11) 3 times, P1, K1 tbl, P1, K3, P1, K1 tbl, P1, †K1, K2tog, yo, K17, yo, sl 1, K1, psso, K1, †P1, K1 tbl, P1, K3, P1, K1 tbl, P1, (K11, P1) 3 times, K13[17:21].
21st row K13[17:21], (P1, K11) 3 times, P1, K1 tbl, P1, T3, P1, K1 tbl, P1, †K23, †P1, K1 tbl, P1, T3, P1, K1 tbl, P1, (K11, P1) 3 times, K13[17:21].
23rd row K13[17:21], (P1, K11) 3 times, P1, K1 tbl, P1, K3, P1, K1 tbl, P1, †K23, †P1, K1 tbl, P1, K3, P1, K1 tbl, P1, (K11, P1) 3 times, K13[17:21].
24th row As 2nd row.
These 24 rows form pat.
Cont without shaping in pat until back measures 22[24:26]", ending with a WS row.

Divide for back opening

Next row Pat 69[73:77] sts, turn and leave rem sts on a spare needle.
Cont without shaping until back measures 26[28:30]", ending with a RS row.

Neck shaping

Next row Bind off 15[16:17] sts pat to end.
Dec one st at neck edge on every foll row until 46[49:52] sts rem.
Cont without shaping until back measures 28[30:32]", ending with a WS row.
Bind off.
With RS facing rejoin yarn to rem sts, K2 tog, pat to end.
Work to match first side, reversing shaping.

■ FRONT

Work as for back until front measures 24[26:28]" *without* dividing sts for back opening, ending with a WS row.

Neck shaping

Next row Pat 56[59:62] sts, turn and leave rem sts on a spare needle.
Dec one st at neck edge on every foll row until 46[49:52] sts rem.
Cont without shaping until front measures 28[30:32]".
Bind off.
With RS facing, rejoin yarn to rem sts and bind off center 27[29:31] sts, pat to end.
Work to match first side, reversing shaping.

■ SLEEVES

Using smaller needles, cast on 58 sts and work in rib as for back until sleeve measures 2", ending with a RS row.
Inc row Rib 3, (M1, rib 4) 5 times, (M1, rib 3) 5 times. (M1, rib 4) 5 times, 73 sts.
Change to larger needles and pat, placing first row as foll:
1st row K4, P1, K11, P1, K1 tbl, P1, T3, P1, K1 tbl, P1, †K11, yo, K2tog, K10, †P1, K1 tbl, P1, T3, P1, K1 tbl, P1, K11, P1, K4.
Cont in pat as set working lace panel in center of sleeve and one rib only at each side, **and at the same time** shape sides by inc one st at each end of 3rd and every 4th row until there are 153 sts, working all inc sts in St st.

Cont without shaping until sleeve measures 19", ending with a WS row.
Next row (RS) P.
Bind off.

■ BACK BUTTONHOLE BAND
With RS facing and using smaller needles, pick up and K32 sts up left edge of back opening.
Next row *K10, yo, K2tog, rep from * once, K to end.
Next row K.
Bind off.

■ BACK BUTTONBAND
Work as for buttonhole band omitting buttonholes.

■ NECKBAND
Join shoulder seams.
With RS facing and using smaller needles, pick up and K35 sts up left back neck, 34 sts down left front neck, 26[28:30] sts across front, 34 sts up right front neck, 35 sts down right back neck. 164[166:168] sts.
Next row K to last 4 sts, K2tog, yo, K2.
Next row K.
Bind off.

■ FINISHING
Fold bound-off edge of sleeves in half and place this point at shoulder seam. Sew edge of sleeves to front and back. Make sure that purl row on sleeves is showing on right side of work.
Join side and sleeve seams.
Sew on buttons.

These samples show the small lace V pattern in gray and the original pattern in salmon pink.

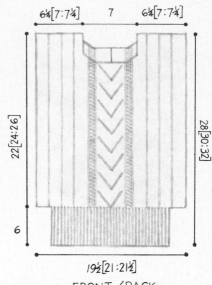
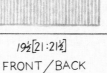

FRONT / BACK

6¼[7:7¼] 7 6¼[7:7¼]

22[24:26]

28[30:32]

6

19½[21:21½]

SLEEVE

21½

19 17

2

10¼

All measurements are in inches

LACE PANEL VARIATION

This classic sweater can be given a different look by knitting a smaller version of the lace stitch. All you need to do is replace the stitches between † and † in the main pattern with the following pattern.

■ SMALL LACE V
1st row K11, yo, K2tog, K10.
2nd row and every alternate row P.
3rd row K9, K2tog, yo, K1, yo, sl 1, K1, psso, K9.

5th row K8, K2tog, yo, K3, yo, sl 1, K1, psso, K8.
7th row K7, K2tog, yo, K5, yo, sl 1, K1, psso, K7.
9th, 11th, 13th, 15th rows K.
These 16 rows form pat.

BALLOONS

The pastel colors within the balloon shapes on this long sweater are knitted in five shades so that balloons seem to rise against the natural background. Reducing the length and leaving off the ribbing converts the design into a T-shirt.

■ SIZE

One size to fit up to 36" bust
See diagram for finished measurements.

■ MATERIALS

Use a lightweight cotton yarn double throughout and light and medium weight yarns for contrast.
22oz/600g main color A (11oz/300g white, 11oz/300g cream – natural)

10oz/250g first contrast B (4oz/100g dark, 2oz/50g medium, 2oz/50g light & 2oz/50g pale orange)
14oz/350g 2nd contrast C (6oz/150g dark, 4oz/100g medium, 2oz/50g light & 2oz/50g pale pink)
14oz/350g 3rd contrast D (4oz/100g dark, 4oz/100g medium, 4oz/100g light & 2oz/50g pale green)
8oz/200g 4th contrast E (2oz/50g dark, 2oz/50g medium, 2oz/50g light & 2oz/50g pale turquoise)
14oz/350g 5th contrast F (2oz/50g dark, 4oz/100g medium, 4oz/100g light & 4oz/100g pale blue)
One pair each of size 7 and 10 knitting needles (or circular knitting needle if preferred) *or size to obtain correct gauge*
One size B crochet hook
Bobbins

■ GAUGE

15 sts and 19 rows to 4" over St st using larger needles
To save time, take time to check gauge.

Note

Do not carry colors across; use a separate bobbin of yarn for each color section. When changing colors, pick up new color from under dropped color to prevent holes (see page 114). Read chart from right to left for RS knit rows and left to right for WS purl rows. Unless stated St st is used throughout. This garment is worked in one piece. The colors of each balloon are indicated on the layout of the dress. The yarns are then used either double or two mixed to achieve the 4 shades for each motif. The background yarn is

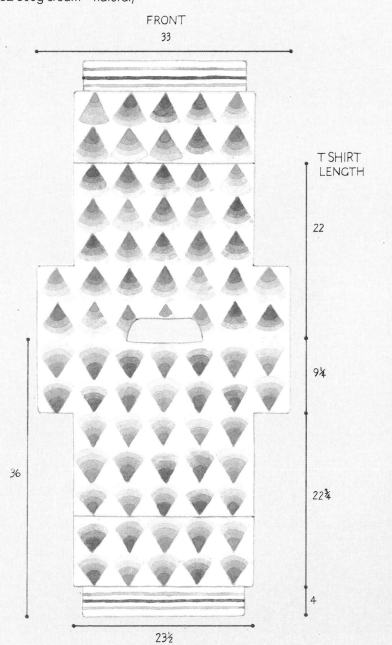

FRONT
33
T SHIRT LENGTH
22
9¼
22¾
4
36
23½
BACK

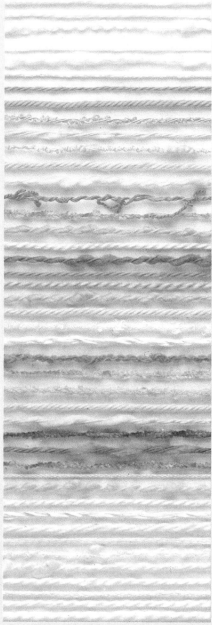

used either double or mixed so as to give as much variation in color and texture as possible.

■ BODY
Back
Using smaller needles and natural, cast on 77 sts and work in rib as foll:
1st rib row (RS) K1, *P1, K1, rep from * to end.
2nd rib row P1, *K1, P1, rep from * to end.
Rep last 2 rows for 27 rows, working next 3 rows in natural, 3 rows in med blue, 5 rows natural, 3 rows med pink, 5 rows natural, 3 rows med green and 5 rows natural, ending with a first row.
Inc row Using natural, rib 6 (M1, rib 6) 3 times, (M1, rib 5) 7 times, (M1, rib 6) 3 times. 90 sts.
Change to larger needles and work without shaping from chart, rep rows 1 to 44 until the end of row 106.

Sleeve shaping
Cast on 18 sts at beg of next 2 rows. 126 sts.
Cont without shaping until end of row 154.

Back neck shaping
Next row Pat 51 sts, turn and leave rem sts on a spare needle.
Next row Bind off 7 sts, pat to end. 44 sts. (This row forms top of shoulder.)
Work 4 rows without shaping, working down graph from row 24 (so that the balloons are reversed).

Front neck shaping
**Inc one st at neck edge on next row.
Cast on 2 sts at beg of next row.
Work one row.
Cast on 3 sts at beg of next row.
Work one row.
Cast on 5 sts at beg of next row.**
Work one row. 55 sts.
Rejoin yarn to rem sts, bind off center 24 sts and pat to end.
Work one row. Bind off 7 sts at beg of next row, pat to end. 44 sts. Work 4 rows without shaping. Rep from ** to ** as first side, ending with a K row.
Next row P to end, turn and cast on 16 sts, turn and P sts from spare needle. 126 sts.
Cont without shaping until 50 rows have been worked from top of shoulder.

Cap shaping
Bind off 18 sts at beg of next 2 rows. 90 sts.
Cont without shaping until front matches back, ending with row 24 of pat.
Next row (K2tog, P1, [K1, P1] twice) 12 times, K2tog, (P1, K1) twice. 77 sts.
Work rib in stripes as for back.
Bind off loosely in rib.

■ SLEEVE EDGES
With RS facing and using smaller needles and natural, pick up and K91 sts evenly along edge of sleeve.
Knit one row.
Work 8 rows in St st, beg with a K row.
Bind off loosely.

■ NECK EDGING
Using crochet hook and natural yarn singly, work one row of single crochet evenly around neck edge.

■ FINISHING
Following manufacturer's directions, block work to finished measurements (see page 118).
Join side and sleeve seams.
Catch down sleeve edges onto WS.

T-SHIRT VERSION
■ BODY
Work as for dress version, omitting rib rows from ** to ** and omitting first 2 rows of balloons.

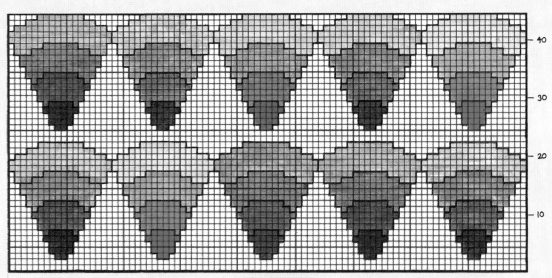

PATTERN CHART

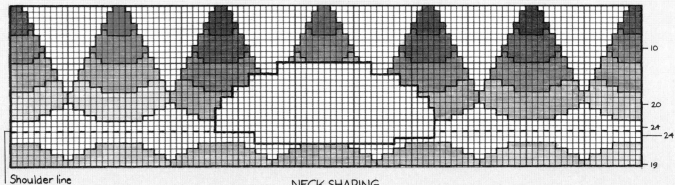

Shoulder line   NECK SHAPING

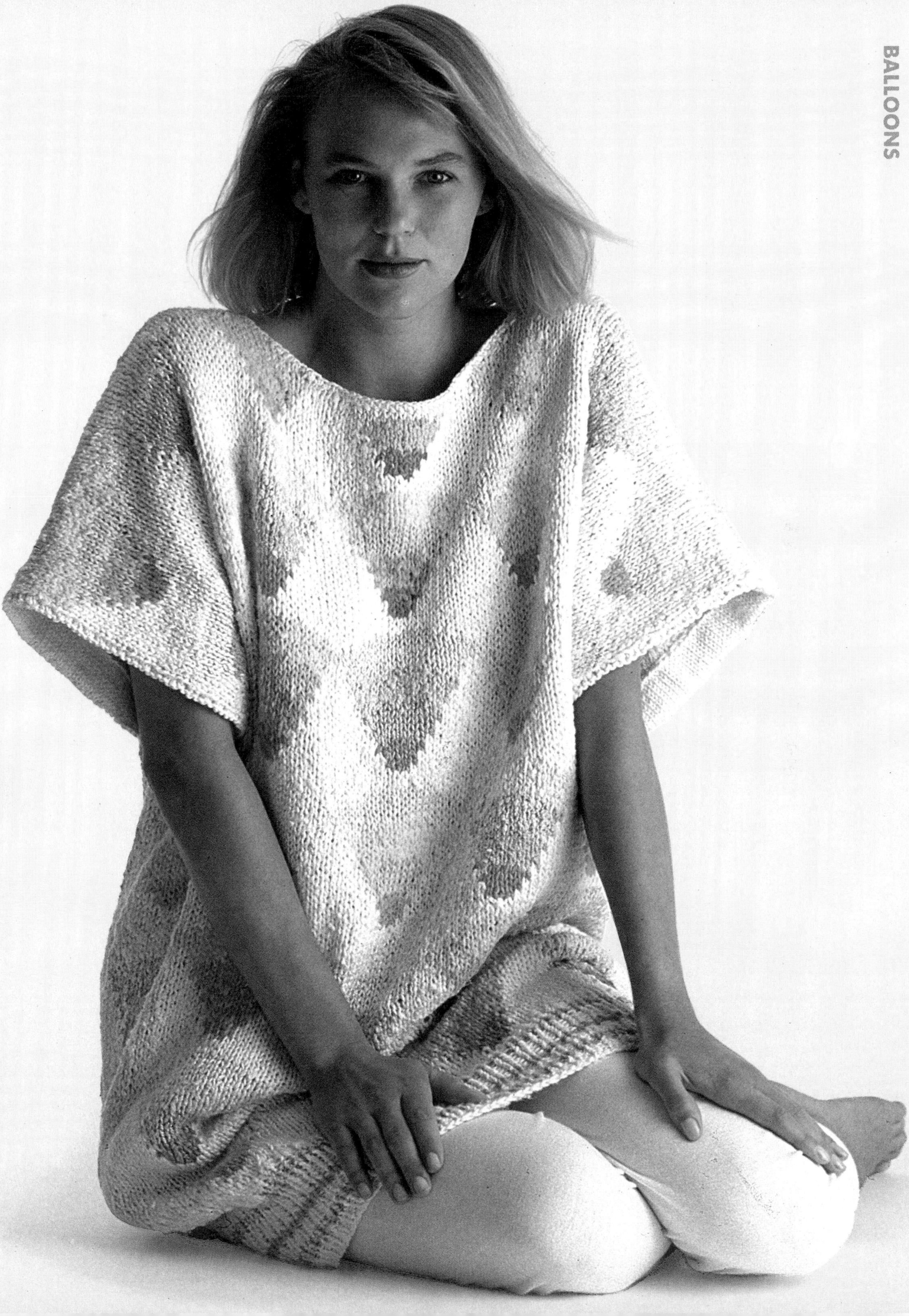

BALLOONS

SPORTY STRIPES

Clear blue and white stripes give a sporty feeling to this loose shirt-style sweater. You could adapt it by knitting in wider stripes, using more color combinations or reducing the stripes and knitting the ribbing, band and collar in a single color.

■ SIZE

One size to fit up to 38" bust
See diagram for finished measurements.

■ MATERIALS

Use a lightweight cotton slub yarn.
15oz/400g color A (blue)
15oz/400g color B (white)
One pair each of sizes 2 and 3 knitting needles *or size to obtain correct gauge*
Three ⅝" buttons

■ GAUGE

32 sts and 32 rows to 4" over pat using larger needles
To save time, take time to check gauge.

■ BACK

Using smaller needles and B, cast on 168 sts and work in rib as foll:
1st rib row *K3A, P3B, rep from * to end.
2nd rib row *K3B, P3A, rep from * to end.
Rep last 2 rows 3 times.
Change to larger needles and work in pat as foll:
1st row *K3B, K3A, rep from * to end.
2nd row P1B, *P3A, P3B, rep from * to last 5 sts, P3A, P2B.
3rd row K1B, *K3A, K3B, rep from * to last 5 sts, K3A, K2B.
4th row *P3B, P3A, rep from * to end.
5th row K2A, *K3B, K3A, rep from * to last 4 sts, K3B, K1A,
6th row P2A, *P3B, P3A, rep from * to last 4 sts, P3B, P1A.
These 6 rows form pat.
Cont in pat without shaping until back measures 17", ending with a WS row.

Armhole shaping

Bind off 8 sts at beg of next 2 rows. 152 sts.
Cont without shaping until back measures 24½", ending with a WS row.

Neck shaping

Next row Pat 56 sts, turn and leave rem sts on a spare needle.
Dec one st at neck edge on next and 3 foll alternate rows. 52 sts.
Bind off using A.
With RS facing, rejoin yarn to rem sts, bind off center 40 sts, pat to end.
Work to match first side, reversing shaping.

■ FRONT

Work as for back until front measures 14¾", ending with a WS row.

Front opening

Next row Pat 80 sts, pick up 8 sts for button band by picking up loop of previous row at back of next 8 sts, turn and leave rem sts on a spare needle. 88 sts.
Working these 8 sts in K1A, P1B rib and rem sts in pat, cont without shaping until front matches back to armhole, ending with a WS row.

Armhole shaping

Bind off 8 sts at beg of next row. 80 sts.
Cont without shaping in pats as set until front measures 36 rows less than back, ending with a RS row.

Neck shaping

Bind off 16 sts at beg of next row. 64 sts.
Dec one st at neck edge of next and 5 foll alternate rows. 58 sts.
Work 3 rows.
Dec one st at neck edge of next and 5 foll 4th rows. 52 sts.
Bind off using A.
Mark positions for 3 buttons on button band.
Rejoin yarn to rem 88 sts and work to match first side, reversing shapings and working 3 buttonholes opposite button positions as foll:
1st buttonhole row Rib 3, bind off 2 sts, rib to end.
2nd buttonhole row Rib, casting on 2 sts over those bound off on previous row.

■ SLEEVES

Using smaller needles and B, cast on 66 sts and work in rib as for back for 2¼", inc one st in last row. 67 sts.
Change to larger needles and cont in pat as set, shaping sides by inc one st at each end of every 3rd row until there are 155 sts and sleeve measures approx 19".

Cap shaping

Dec one st at each end of next and 3 foll alternate rows. 147 sts.
Bind off using A.

■ COLLAR

Join shoulder seams.
With RS facing and A, pick up and K41 sts up right front neck, 61 sts around back neck and 41 sts down left front neck omitting tops of bands. 143 sts.
Work in K1A, P1B rib as for button band for 2¾".
Bind off loosely in rib using A.

■ POCKET

Using larger needles and B, cast on 40 sts and work 5" in diagonal stripe pat. Change to smaller needles and work in K1A, P1B rib for ¾". Bind off loosely in rib using A.

■ FINISHING

Following manufacturer's directions, block pieces to finished measurements (see page 118).
Place center of bound-off edge of sleeve at shoulder seam and join to back and front. Join side and sleeve seams.
Sew on pocket in desired position.
Sew on buttons.

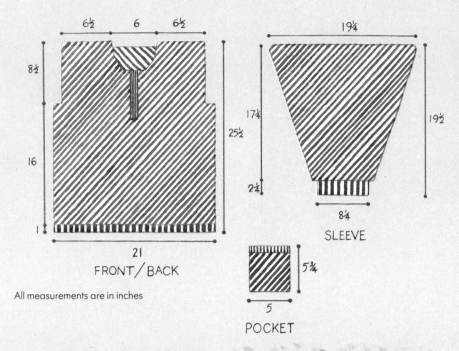

FRONT/BACK

All measurements are in inches

SLEEVE

POCKET

STRIPE VARIATION

You could make the stripe wider by knitting six stitches in each diagonal stripe instead of three. If so, the first row of the back will then be worked as *K6B, K6A, rep from * to end. Or you can change the color scheme by using more than two colors: here the master pattern has been knitted in gray, yellow and white. Using three colors, with the yarn woven in at the back of the work, creates a more tightly woven — and consequently a warmer — fabric.

38

CABLE CLASSIC

An elegant classic shape with a cable, this cardigan is a timeless design that would suit almost anybody.

■ SIZE

To fit 32-34[36-38:40-42]" bust
Figures for larger sizes are given in brackets. Where there is only one set of figures, this applies to all sizes.
See diagram for finished measurements.

■ MATERIALS

18[20:22]oz/500[550:600]g fine mercerized cotton yarn
One pair each of sizes 2 and 4 knitting needles *or size to obtain correct gauge*
Four ⅝" buttons
One cable needle

■ GAUGE

28 sts and 38 rows to 4" over St st using larger needles
To save time, take time to check gauge.

Note
Slip first stitch and knit last stitch on every row to insure a firm edge.

■ BACK

Using smaller needles, cast on 121[127:133] sts.
**1st rib row (RS) K to end, working into back of every st.
2nd rib row P1, *K1, P1, rep from * to end.
3rd rib row K1, P1, K1, rep from * to end.
Rep last 2 rows until rib measures 4", ending with a 3rd row.**
Inc row P4, (M1, P4) 4[6:8] times, (M1, P5) 17[15:13] times, (M1, P4) 4[6:8] times. 146[154:162] sts.
Change to larger needles and work in pat as foll:
1st row (RS) K13[17:21], *P3, K9, P3*, K90, rep from * to * once, K13[17:21].
2nd row and every alternate row P13[17:21], *K1, P1, K1, P9, K1, P1, K1*, P90, rep from * to * once, P13[17:21].
3rd row K13[17:21], *P3, slip 3 sts onto cable needle and hold at front of work, K3, then K3 from cable needle – called CF6 –, K3, P3*, K90, rep from * to * once, K13[17:21].
5th row As first row.
7th row K13[17:21], *P3, K3, slip 3 sts onto cable needle and hold at back of work, K3, then K3 from cable needle – called CB6 –, P3*, K90, rep from * to * once, K13[17:21].

The stitch pattern is knitted in a different color but in the same mercerized cotton as the pale green on page 41.

8th row As 2nd row.
These 8 rows form pat.
Cont in pat without shaping until back measures 23½[25½:27½]", ending with a RS row.
Bind off.

■ RIGHT FRONT

Using smaller needles, cast on 49[51:53] sts and work as for back from ** to **.
Inc row P3, (M1, P4) 5[3:1] times, (M1, P3) 2[8:14] times, (M1, P4) 5[3:1] times. 61[65:69] sts.
Change to larger needles and work in pat as foll:
1st row K33, P3, K9, P3, K13[17:21].
2nd and every alternate row P13[17:21], K1, P1, K1, P9, K1, P1, K1, P33.

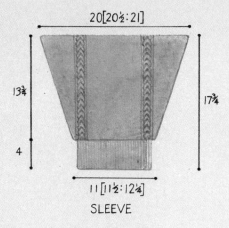

20[20½:21]

13¾

17¾

4

11[11½:12¼]

SLEEVE

All measurements are in inches

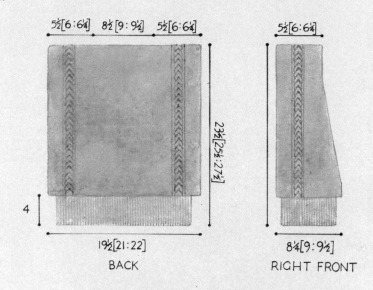

5½[6:6¼] 8½[9:9½] 5½[6:6¼]

5½[6:6¼]

23½[25½:27½]

4

19½[21:22]

BACK

8¼[9:9½]

RIGHT FRONT

3rd row K33, P3, C6F, K3, P3, K13[17:21].
5th row As first row.
7th row K33, P3, K3, C6B, P3, K13[17:21].
8th row As 2nd row.
These 8 rows form pat.
Cont in pat without shaping until front measures 5", ending with a RS row.

Front shaping
Dec one st at beg of next and every foll 8th row until 43[45:47] sts rem. Cont without shaping until front measures 23½[25½:27½]".
Bind off.

■ LEFT FRONT
Work as for right front, reversing shaping and placing first row of pat as foll:
1st row K13[17:21], P3, K9, P3, K33.

■ SLEEVES
Using smaller needles, cast on 59 sts and work as back from ** to **.
Inc row P3, (M1, P1) 0[3:7] times, (M1, P2) 26[24:20] times, (M1, P1) 0[3:7] times, P4[2:2]. 85[89:93] sts.
Change to larger needles and work in pat as for back, placing first row as foll:
1st row K3, *P3, K9, P3*, K49[53:57], rep from * to * once, K3.
Cont in pat, shaping sides by inc one st at each end of 3rd and every foll 4th row until there are 147[151:155] sts, working extra sts in St st.

Work without shaping until sleeve measures 17¾", ending with a WS row.
Next row (RS) P.
Bind off.

■ FRONT BANDS AND COLLAR
Using smaller needles, cast on 39 sts.
1st row (RS) K to end, working into back of every st.
2nd row K2, *P1, K1, rep from * to last st, K1.
3rd row K1, *P1, K1, rep from * to end.
Rep last 2 rows twice.
1st buttonhole row Rib 8, bind off 2 sts, rib 19, bind off 2 sts, rib 8.
2nd buttonhole row Rib, casting on 2 sts over those bound off on previous row.
Cont in rib until band measures 5".
Work the 2 buttonhole rows once more.
Cont in rib until band when slightly stretched fits up right front, across back neck and down left front.
Bind off.

■ FINISHING
Join shoulder seams.
Mark central point of back neck and ribbed collar.
Place collar at center of back neck and sew evenly to right and left fronts with buttonholes at bottom of right front.
Place center of bound-off edge of sleeves at shoulder seams and join sleeves to back and front evenly.
Join side and sleeve seams.
Sew on buttons.

40

CABBAGE ROSE

The simple scattered motif of a cabbage rose offers possibilities for completely different effects, depending on the yarns chosen. The fleck yarn has an earthy appeal, whereas a white yarn creates a more sophisticated look (see page 46).

■ SIZE

To fit 34[36:38-40]" bust
Figures for larger sizes are given in brackets. Where there is only one set of figures, this applies to all sizes.
See diagram for finished measurements.

■ MATERIALS

Use a fine cotton yarn knitted double for the main color and a medium weight cotton yarn for contrast.
25[27:29]oz/700[750:800]g main color A (brown fleck)
3oz/70g contrast B (green)
1oz/25g each C, D, E and F (blue, yellow, pink, beige)
One pair each of sizes 4 and 7 knitting needles *or size to obtain correct gauge*

■ GAUGE

18 sts and 26 rows to 4" over St st using larger needles
To save time, take time to check gauge.

Note

Read chart from right to left for RS knit rows and left to right for WS purl rows.
Main color fleck yarn is knitted double throughout. To knit the white garment, use a medium weight cotton knitted singly.
Do not carry colors for rose motif across; use a separate length of yarn for each color section. When changing colors, pick up new color from under dropped color to prevent holes. Weave main color across back of motif (see page 114).

■ BACK

Using smaller needles and A, cast on 69[71:75] sts and work in rib as foll:
1st rib row (RS) K1, *P1, K1, rep from * to end.
2nd rib row P1, *K1, P1, rep from * to end.
Rep last 2 rows until rib measures 3", ending with a first row.
Inc row Rib 3[1:3], (M1, rib 3) 4[2:1] times, (M1, rib 2) 21[29:33] times, (M1, rib 3) 4[2:1] times. 98[104:110] sts.
Change to larger needles and St st and work in pat from row 1 of body chart for 54 rows.

Armhole shaping

Dec one st at each end of next and every foll alternate row to end of row 126[130:134]. 26[28:30] sts.
Bind off.

■ FRONT

Work as for back to end of row 114 [114:116], but do not work top flower motif. 38[44:50] sts.

Neck shaping

Next row K2tog, pat 10[13:16] sts, turn and leave rem sts on a spare needle.
Work one row.
Dec one st at each end of next and every alternate row to 3[2:3] sts.
Work one row.
2nd size:
K2tog and fasten off.
First and 3rd sizes:
Sl 1, K2tog, psso, fasten off.

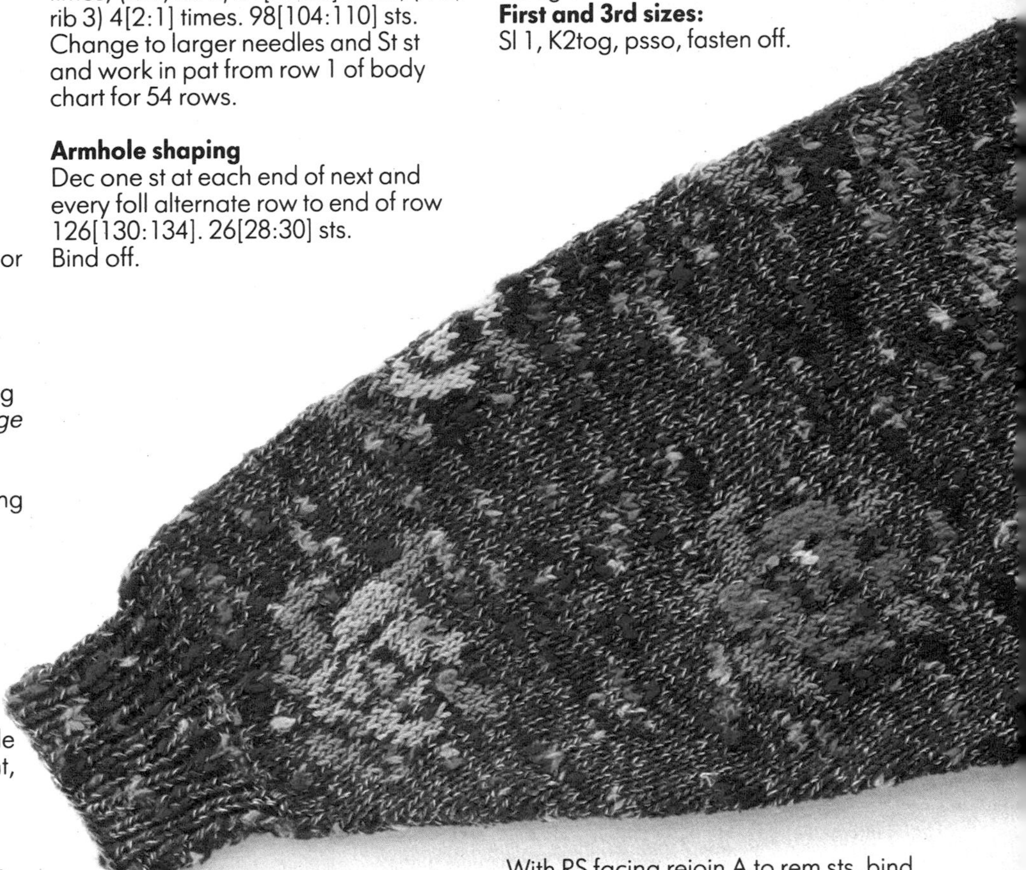

With RS facing rejoin A to rem sts, bind off center 14 sts and work to match first side, reversing all shapings.

■ SLEEVES

Using smaller needles and A, cast on 33[37:41] sts and work in rib as for back for 3", ending with a first row.
Inc row Rib 3, (M1, rib 2) 15[17:19] times. 48[54:60] sts.
Change to larger needles and work in pat from row 1 of sleeve chart, inc one st at each end of 3rd and every foll alternate row to 72[78:84] sts.
Work one row. (row 26)
Inc one st at each end of next and every foll 3rd row to 96[102:108] sts.
Work 6 rows without shaping.
Dec one st at each end of next (row 67) and every foll alternate row 10 times. 76[82:88] sts. (row 85)
Dec one st at each end of next 2 rows.
Next row Pat to end.
Rep last 3 rows to 6[8:10] sts.
Bind off.

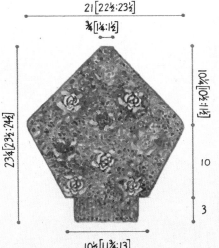

All measurements are in inches

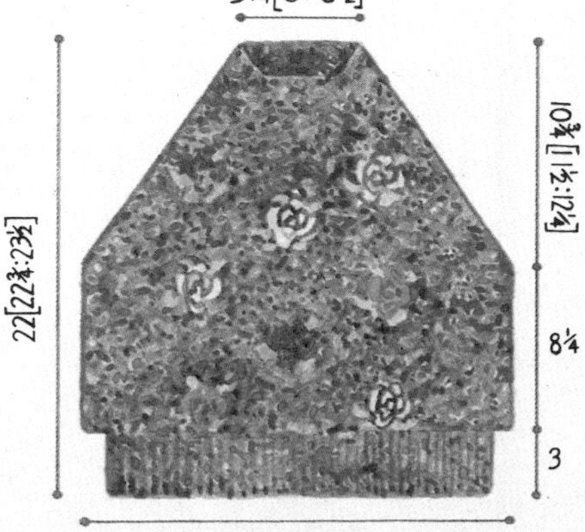

5¾[6:6½]

22[22¼:23¼]
10¾[11½:12¼]
8¼
3

21¼[22¼:23½]
FRONT/BACK

21[22½:23½]
⅜[1¼:1½]
23¾[23½:24¼]
10¾[10½:11½]
10
3

10½[11¾:13]
SLEEVE

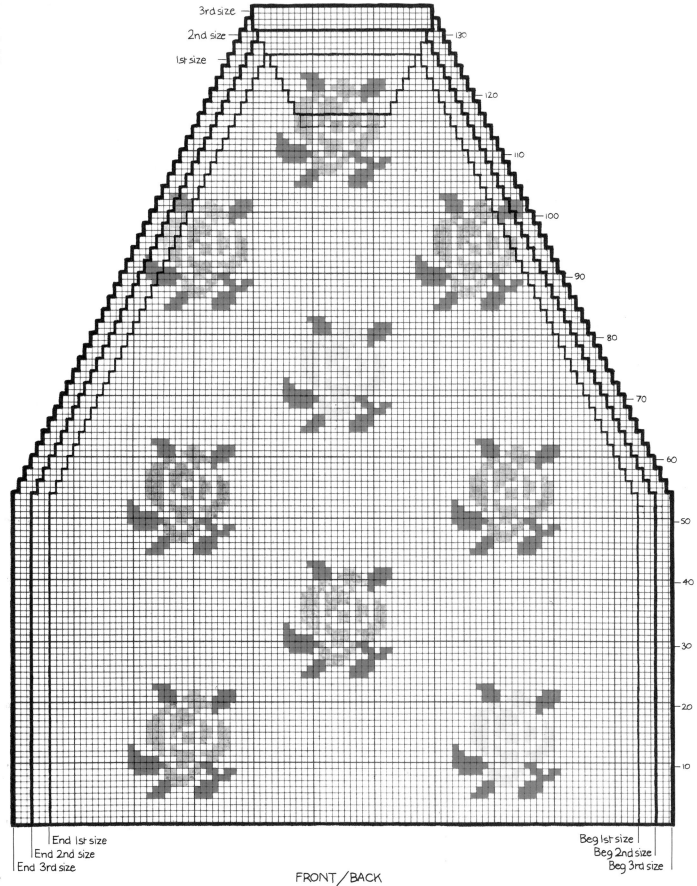

3rd size

2nd size — 130

1st size — 120

— 110

— 100

— 90

— 80

— 70

— 60

— 50

— 40

— 30

— 20

— 10

End 1st size
End 2nd size
End 3rd size

Beg 1st size
Beg 2nd size
Beg 3rd size

44

FRONT / BACK

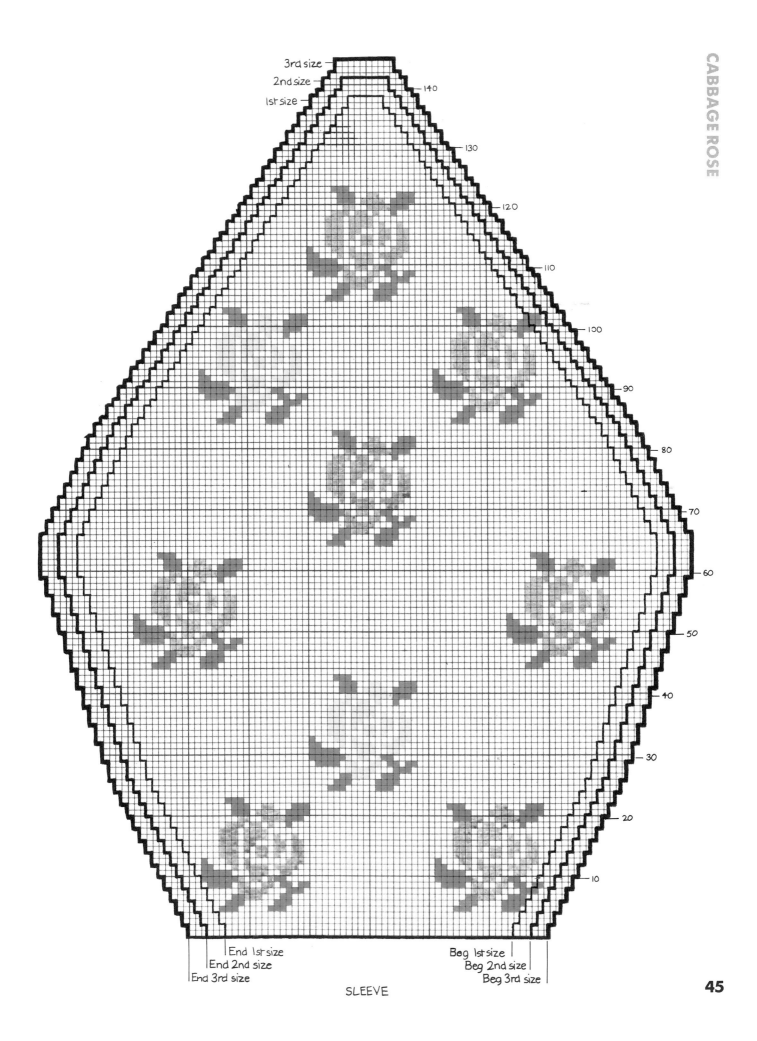

3rd size

2nd size — 140

1st size

— 130

— 120

— 110

— 100

— 90

— 80

— 70

— 60

— 50

— 40

— 30

— 20

— 10

End 1st size

End 2nd size

End 3rd size

Beg 1st size

Beg 2nd size

Beg 3rd size

SLEEVE

■ FINISHING
Raglan ribs (Make 4)
These are worked along shaped
edges of top of raglan sleeves. With RS
facing and using smaller needles and
A, pick up and K61 sts evenly along
shaped edge and work in rib as for
back for 1½".
Bind off loosely in rib.
Join sleeve edges to armhole edges;
leave left back open.

Neckband
With RS facing and using smaller
needles and A, pick up and K4 sts
along raglan rib, 6[8:10] sts across top
of sleeve, 4 sts along raglan rib,
29[35:39] sts around front neck, 4 sts
along raglan rib, 6[8:10] sts at top of
sleeve, 4 sts along raglan rib,
24[26:28] sts across back neck.
81[93:103] sts.
Work in rib as for back for 3".
Bind off loosely in rib.
Darn in ends. Following
manufacturer's directions, block work
to finished measurements (see page
118).
Join rem raglan sleeve and collar
edge. (Join collar on RS.)
Join side and sleeve seams.
Fold neckband in half to outside and
sew in place carefully.

SUGARED ALMOND

JANICE WILKINS

The muted pastel tones soften the stripes in this stylish pullover. The rectangles are worked in stockinette stitch and eyelet stitch.

■ SIZE
To fit 32-34[36-38]" bust
Figures for larger sizes are given in brackets. Where there is only one set of figures, this applies to both sizes.
See diagram for finished measurements.

■ MATERIALS
Use a medium weight cotton yarn.
10[10]oz/260[280]g main color A (white)
7[8]oz/190[210]g 1st contrast B (green)
6[7]oz/160[180]g 2nd contrast C (pale green)
7[8]oz/190[210]g 3rd contrast D (orange)
One pair each of size 3 and 5 knitting needles *or size to obtain correct gauge*

■ GAUGE
24 sts and 28 rows to 4" over St st using larger needles
To save time, take time to check gauge.

Note
For ease of working, the collar may be made in 2 pieces and joined at center back.

■ BACK
Using smaller needles, cast on 24[27] sts with A, 35[38] sts with D, 32[33] sts with C, 24[27] sts with B. 115[125] sts.
Keeping colors correct, work in rib as foll:
1st rib row (RS) K1, *P1, K1, rep from * to end.
2nd rib row P1, *K1, P1, rep from * to end.
Rep last 2 rows until rib measures 3", ending with a first row.
Inc row Rib 3, (M1, rib 6) 18[20] times, M1, rib to end. 134[146] sts.
Change to larger needles and beg pat as foll:
1st row (RS) K45[51]A, K27B, (K1A, K1D) 10 times, K42[48]C.
2nd row P42[48]C, (P1D, P1A) 10 times, P27B, P45[51]A.
3rd row K5A, (yo, K2togA, K4A) 6[7] times, yo, K2togA, K2A, K27B, (K1A, K1D) 10 times, K42[48]C.
4th row As 2nd row.
5th and 6th rows As first and 2nd rows.
7th row K2A, (yo, K2togA, K4A) 7[8] times, K1A, K27B, (K1A, K1D) 10 times, K42[48]C.
8th row As 2nd row.
Last 8 rows form pat for first strip of color rectangles.

Cont in pat as set until 25[27] rows have been completed.
Beg 2nd strip of color rectangles as foll:
1st row (WS) P37[43]B, P33A, P32D, (P1A, P1D) 16[19] times.
2nd row (K1D, K1A) 16[19] times, K32D, K33A, K5B, (yo, K2togB, K4B) 4[5] times, yo, K2togB, K6B.
3rd row As first row.
4th row (K1D, K1A) 16[19] times, K32D, K33A, K37[43]B.
5th row As first row.
6th row (K1D, K1A) 16[19] times, K32D, K33A, K2B, (yo, K2togB, K4B) 5[6] times, yo, K2togB, K3B.
7th row As first row.
8th row As 4th row.
Last 8 rows form pat for 2nd strip of color rectangles.
Cont in pat as set until 25[27] rows of this strip have been completed.
Beg 3rd strip of color rectangles as foll:
1st row (RS) K42[48]B, K32C, (K1B, K1D) 15 times, K30[36]A.
2nd row P30[36]A, (P1D, P1B) 15 times, P32C, P42[48]B.
3rd row K42[48]B, K5C,(yo, K2togC, K4C) 4 times, yo, K2togC, K1C, (K1B, K1D) 15 times, K30[36]A.
4th row As 2nd row.
5th and 6th rows As first and 2nd rows.
7th row K42[48]B, K2C, (yo, K2togC, K4C) 5 times, (K1B, K1D) 15 times, K30[36]A.
8th row As 2nd row.
Last 8 rows form pat for 3rd strip of color rectangles.
Cont in pat as set until 25[27] rows have been completed, placing a marker at both ends of 23rd[25th] row.
Beg 4th strip of color rectangles as foll:

1st row (WS) P42[48]C, P35D, (P1B, P1C) 12 times, P33[39]A.
2nd row K33[39]A, (K1C, K1B) 12 times, K35D, K5C, (yo, K2togC, K4C) 6[7] times, K1C.
3rd row As first row.
4th row K33[39]A, (K1C, K1B) 12 times, K35D, K42[48]C.
5th row As first row.
6th row K33[39]A, (K1C, K1B) 12 times, K35D, K2C, (yo, K2togC, K4C) 6[7] times, yo, K2togC, K3C.
7th row As first row.
8th row As 4th row.
Last 8 rows form pat for 4th strip of color rectangles.
Cont in pat as set until 25[27] rows have been completed.
Beg 5th strip of color rectangles as foll:
1st row (RS) K27[33]D, K36C, K25A, (K1D, K1A) 23[26] times.
2nd row (P1A, P1D) 23[26] times, P25A, P36C, P27[33]D.
3rd row K27[33]D, K5C, (yo, K2togC,K4C) 5 times, K1C, K25A, (K1D, K1A) 23[26] times.
4th row As 2nd row.
5th and 6th rows As first and 2nd rows.
7th row K27[33]D, K2C, (yo, K2togC, K4C) 5 times, yo, K2togC, K2C, K25A, (K1D, K1A) 23[26] times.
8th row As 2nd row.
Last 8 rows form pat for 5th strip of color rectangles.
Cont in pat as set until 25[27] rows have been completed.
Beg 6th strip of color rectangles as foll:
1st row (WS) P18[24]B, P44D, (P1A, P1B) 14 times, P44[50]A.

By replacing the four pastel colors with a monochromatic scheme, the bricklike build up of rectangles on this design produces a more austere and striking garment.

2nd row K44[50]A, (K1B, K1A) 14 times, K5D, (yo, K2togD, K4D) 6 times, yo, K2togD, K1D, K18[24]B.
3rd row As first row.
4th row K44[50]A, (K1D, K1A) 14 times, K32D, K44D, K18[24]B.
5th row As first row.
6th row K44[50]A, (K1D, K1A) 14 times, K2D, (yo, K2togD, K4D) 7 times, K18[24]B.
7th row As first row.
8th row As 4th row.
Last 8 rows form pat for 6th strip of color rectangles.
Cont in pat as set until 25[29] rows have been completed.
Bind off.

■ FRONT

Work as for back until 70[76] rows of pat have been worked.

Neck shaping
Next row Pat 66[72] sts, turn and leave rem sts on a spare needle.
Work 2 rows.
Place a marker at both ends of last row.
Dec one st at neck edge on next and every foll 3rd row until 45[51] sts rem.
Cont without shaping until front measures same as back to shoulder.
Bind off.
With RS facing, rejoin yarn to rem sts, bind off 2 sts, pat to end.
Work to match first side, reversing shaping.

■ SLEEVES

Using smaller needles, cast on 24 sts with D and 21 sts with C. 45 sts.
Work in rib as for back for 2¾".
Inc row Rib 3, (M1, rib 3) 13 times, rib 3. 58 sts.
Change to larger needles and beg pat as foll:
1st row (RS) K7A, K27B, (K1A, K1D) 10 times, K4C.

Last row sets position of strips as for center 58 sts of back.
Cont in pat as set for back, inc one st at each end of 3rd and every foll 3rd row until there are 134 sts.
Cont in pat without shaping until sleeve measures 18½".
Bind off.

■ COLLAR

Using larger needles and A, cast on 242 sts and using A and B work in St st and 2 color stripe pat for 26 rows.
Using A only, work 4 more rows.
Bind off.

■ FINISHING

Following manufacturer's directions, block pieces to finished measurements (see page 118).
Join shoulder seams.
Sew bound-off edge of sleeve between markers on back and front.
Join side and sleeve seams.
Turn plain edge of collar to WS and sew to form hem.
Sew collar evenly to neck edge.

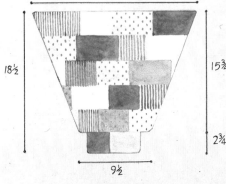

7½[8½]   7   7½[8½]

10½

8½

3

22

22[24]

FRONT/BACK

22

18½   15¾

2¾

9½

SLEEVE

All measurements are in inches

RACING COLORS

Vivid streaks of color bring this black and green checked sweater to life. The garment has deep armholes and is designed to be worn over another top. You could sew up part of the armholes to reduce the depth.

■ SIZE

To fit 34-36[38-40]" bust
Figures for larger sizes are given in brackets. Where there is only one set of figures, this applies to all sizes.
See diagram for finished measurements.

■ MATERIALS

Use a medium weight cotton yarn.
13[15]oz/350[400]g main color A (black)
9oz/250g first contrast B (olive green)
2oz/50g each in 3 contrasting colors C, D and E (yellow, orange, pale blue)
One pair of size 6 knitting needles
One 16"-long size 7 circular knitting needle
One 24"-long size 7 circular needle, *or size to obtain correct gauge.*
Stitch holder

The darts of color make a bold statement across this sleeveless tunic. This variation has an off-beat background check of orange and brown with a beautiful bright focus in the turquoise, yellow and lime green.

■ GAUGE

20 sts and 22 rows to 4" over check pat using larger needles
To save time, take time to check gauge.

Note

When working check pat, carry color not in use loosely across wrong side of work (see page 114).
Back and front are each worked back and forth in rows on a circular needle so that two RS rows or two WS rows can be worked one after another by sliding sts to other end of needle and working back across them in the same direction as the last row.

■ BACK

** Using A and smaller needles, cast on 104[108] sts and work in rib as foll:
1st rib row *K4, P4, rep from * to end.
Rep last row 9 times.
Change to longer circular needle and beg check pat, working back and forth in rows as foll:
1st row (RS) *K2 in A, K2 in B, rep from * to end.
2nd row *P2 in B, P2 in A, rep from * to end.
3rd and 4th rows As first and 2nd rows.
5th row *K2 in B, K2 in A, rep from * to end.
6th row *P2 in A, P2 in B, rep from * to end.
7th and 8th rows As 5th and 6th rows.
These 8 rows form check pat.
Beg first short stripe as foll:
9th row Using C only, K44 sts, turn and leave rem sts unworked.
10th row Sl 1, P to end
11th row K42, turn.
12th row As 10th row.
13th row K40, turn.
14th row As 10th row.
15th to 22nd rows As first—8th rows.

All measurements are in inches

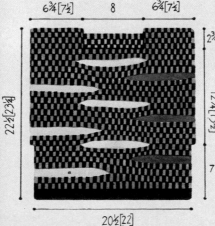

6¾[7½]   8   6¾[7½]

2¾

22½[23¼]   12¾[13½]

7

20½[22]

FRONT / BACK

23rd row Slide all sts to other end of needle and with WS facing and using D only, P44 sts, turn and leave rem sts unworked.
24th row Sl 1, K to end.
25th row P42, turn.
26th row As 24th row.
27th row P40, turn.
28th row As 24th row.
29th to 36th rows Slide all sts to other end of needle and beg with RS facing, work as for first-8th rows.
37th row Slip first 30[34] sts onto RH needle, using E, K44, turn.
38th row Sl 1, P42, turn.
39th row Sl 1, K40, turn.
40th row Sl 1, P38, turn.
41st row Sl 1, K36, turn.
42nd row Sl 1, P34, turn.
Rep these 42 rows twice, **and at the same time** inc 2 sts at beg of first and 2nd rows only (108[116] sts) and work 2 extra sts in C and D stripes and slip 2 extra sts onto RH needle on row 37.**
Cont without shaping in check pat only, work 20[24] rows.

Neck shaping

Next row Work first 34[38] sts in check pat, turn and leave rem sts on a spare needle.
Cont without shaping for 9 rows.
Bind off.
With RS facing, slip center 40 sts onto st holder for back neck and rejoin yarns to rem 34[38] sts and work to match first side.

■ FRONT

Work as back from ** to **, but working C stripes on left side of work and D stripes on right side of work, so that short stripes match at side seams.
Cont without shaping in check pat only, work 12[16] rows.

Neck shaping

Next row Work first 34[38] sts in check pat, turn and leave rem sts on a spare needle.
Cont without shaping, work 17 rows.
Bind off.
With RS facing, slip center 40 sts onto st holder for front neck and rejoin yarns to rem 34[38] sts and work to match first side.

■ NECKBAND

Join shoulder seams.
With RS facing and using shorter circular needle, work in check pat across 40 sts of center back from st holder, pick up and pat 16 sts evenly down left side of neck, pat across 40 sts of front neck from st holder, pick up and pat 16 sts evenly up right side of neck. 112 sts.
Work 15 rounds in check pat.
Bind off.

■ ARMBANDS
Join side seams.
With RS facing and using longer circular needle, pick up and K152[156] sts around armhole and work 12 rounds in K2, P2 rib.
Bind off.

■ FINISHING
Following manufacturer's directions, block sweater to finished measurements (see page 118).

WAVEBAND

This generously proportioned T-shaped top flatters any figure. Knitted in black and lurex yarn, it would make a sophisticated evening top.

■ SIZE

One size to fit up to 42" bust
See diagram for finished measurements.

■ MATERIALS

Use a lightweight cotton yarn.
23oz/650g main color A (white)
2oz/50g contrast B (black)
2oz/50g contrast C (orange)
One pair each of sizes 4 and 5 knitting needles *or size to obtain correct gauge*

■ GAUGE

23 sts and 28 rows to 4" over St st using larger needles
To save time, take time to check gauge.

Note

Read chart from right to left for RS knit rows and left to right for WS purl rows. Unless stated St st is used throughout. Do not carry color for thin stripes across; use a separate bobbin of yarn for each color section. When changing colors, pick up new color from under dropped color to prevent holes (see page 114).

■ BACK AND FRONT (alike)

Using smaller needles and A, cast on 139 sts and work in rib as foll:
1st rib row (RS) K1, *P1, K1, rep from * to end.
2nd rib row P1, *K1, P1, rep from * to end.
Rep last 2 rib rows twice, inc one st in last row. 140 sts.
Change to larger needles and work without shaping from row 1 of chart to end of row 98.
Mark both ends of last row for armholes.
Cont without shaping to end of row 168.

Neck shaping

Next row Pat 47 sts, turn and leave rem sts on a spare needle.
Bind off 4 sts at beg of next row.
Work one row.
Bind off 3 sts at beg of next row.
Dec one st at neck edge on next 5 rows. 35 sts.
Cont without shaping to end of chart.
Bind off.
With RS facing, rejoin yarn to rem sts, bind off center 46 sts, pat to end.
Work to match first side, reversing shaping.

■ FIRST SLEEVE

Using smaller needles, cast on 115 sts and work in rib as for back. 116 sts.
Change to larger needles and work in pat from row 1 of sleeve chart, shaping sides by inc one st at each end of every 3rd row until there are 138 sts.
Cont without shaping to end of chart.
Bind off.

■ SECOND SLEEVE

Work as for first sleeve working first stripe in B and 2nd stripe in C.

■ NECKBAND

Join right shoulder.
With RS facing and using larger needles and A, pick up and K63 sts evenly around front neck and 63 sts evenly around back neck. 126 sts.
Beg with a P row, work in St st for 13 rows.
Bind off.

■ FINISHING

Following manufacturer's directions, block pieces to finished measurements (see page 118).
Join left shoulder and neckband.
Sew bound-off edge of sleeves to back and front between markers.
Join side and sleeve seams.

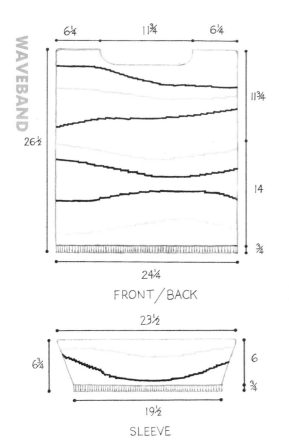

6¼   11¾   6¼

26½

11¾

14

¾

24¼

FRONT / BACK

23½

6¾

6

¾

19½

SLEEVE

All measurements are in inches

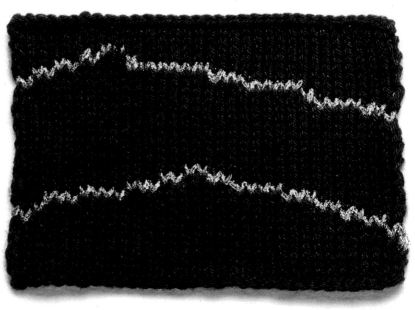

Black cotton yarn and a double strand of lurex change this big T-shirt to a sophisticated garment for evening.

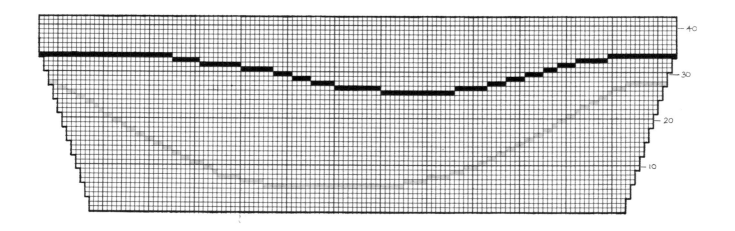

FIRST SLEEVE

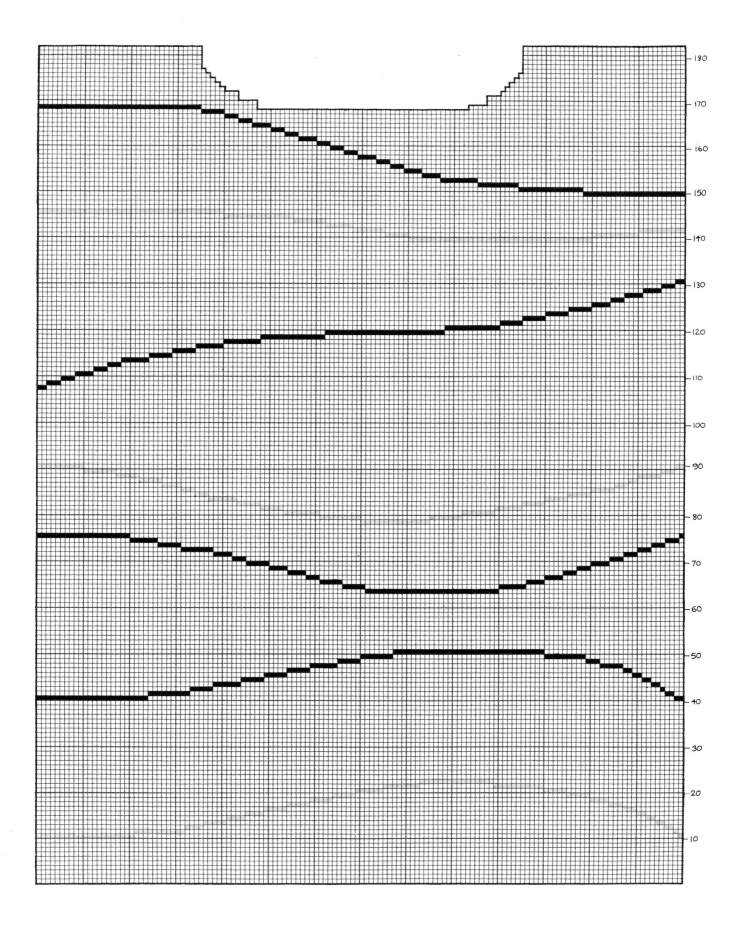

FRONT/BACK

RAZZLE DAZZLE

Multicolored triangles and dots combine in this easy-to-knit summer top. The mixture of garter and stockinette stitch adds texture to this vibrant but simple garment. The shanked buttons are purely decorative.

SIZE
To fit 32-34[36-38]" bust
Figures for larger sizes are given in brackets. Where there is only one set of figures, this applies to all sizes. *See diagram for finished measurements.*

MATERIALS
Use a fine mercerized cotton yarn.
9[11]oz/250[300]g main color A (pink)
2 oz/50g first contrast B (turquoise)
2 oz/50g 2nd contrast C (blue)
One pair each of sizes 3 and 4 knitting needles *or size to obtain correct gauge*
Eight ¾" buttons

GAUGE
24 sts and 46 rows to 4" over garter st using larger needles
To save time, take time to check gauge.

Note
Read chart from right to left for RS odd-numbered rows and left to right for WS even numbered rows.
Use separate ball of yarn for each dot. When changing colors, pick up new color from under dropped color to prevent holes (see page 114).

FRONT AND BACK (alike)
Triangles
Using larger needles and A, cast on 2 sts.
1st row K2.
2nd row Beg row with yarn at front of work and over right hand needle to make a loop – called yo –, K2.
3rd row Yo, K3.
4th row Yo, K4.
Cont in this way until end of row 13. 14 sts. This completes first triangle.
Make 6 triangles more using C for the next triangle, then A, B, A, C, A and beg each triangle by casting the 2 sts onto the tree needle. *Do not break yarn at end of last point.*
Using A only, K across all 98 sts.
1st size only:
Knit 9 rows.
2nd size only:
Knit next 4 rows, working a yo at beg of each row. 102 sts.
Knit one row more.
Both sizes:
Cont without shaping from row 11 of chart, working background in g st and dots in St st.

Foll chart until 148th row has been completed. Knit 8 rows. Front should measure approx 34cm from top of triangles.
Change to smaller needles and using A only, work 10 rows in K1, P1 rib. Bind off loosely in rib.

STRAPS (Make 4)
Using B, cast on 2 sts.
1st row K2.
2nd row Yo, K2.
3rd row Yo, K3.
4th row Yo, K4.
5th row Yo, K5.
6th row Yo, K6.
7th row Yo, K7. 8 sts.
Knit 4 rows without shaping.
Next row K1, P1, K4, P1, K1.
Next row P.
Rep last 2 rows 64 times, or until strap measures desired length.
Knit 4 rows.
K2tog at beg of next and every foll row until 2 sts rem. Bind off.
Make one more strap in B and 2 straps in C.

FINISHING
Following manufacturer's directions, block pieces to finished measurements (see page 118); avoid stretching. Join side seams.

Overlapping strap on front by approx 2", sew one strap in B and one strap in C to each side, placing first strap of each pair 2¼" from side seam and 2nd strap 4¼" from side seam. Cross each pair of straps approx 4¾" from each end and sew tog ar crossings. Sew straps to back in the same way as for front. Sew one button to each strap end.

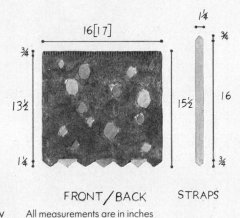

FRONT/BACK   STRAPS

All measurements are in inches

The background color and the contrasts have been changed around on this alternative version.

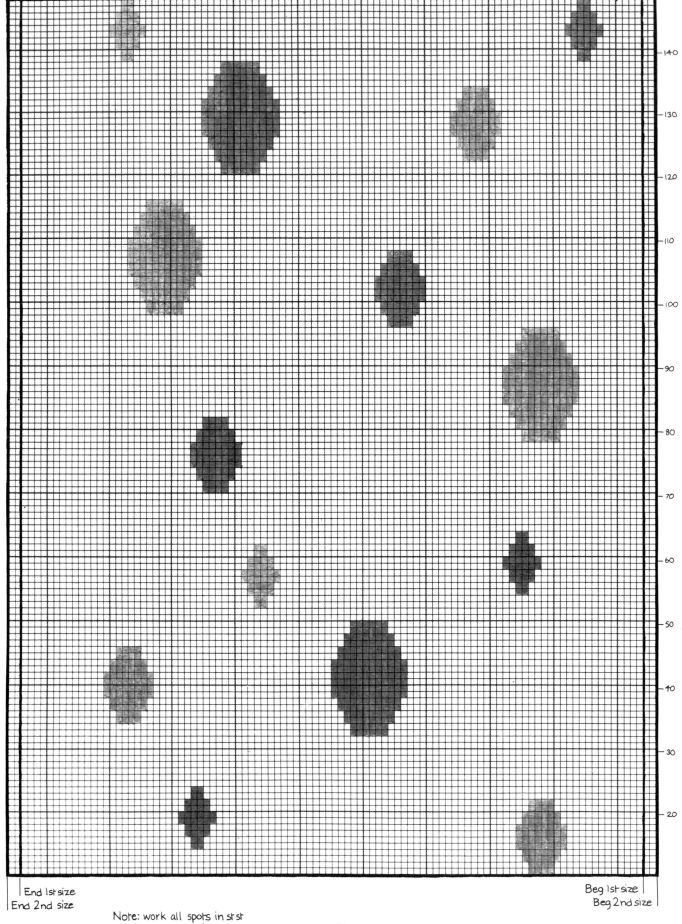

End 1st size
End 2nd size

Beg 1st size
Beg 2nd size

Note: work all spots in st st
and background in garter st   FRONT/BACK

CHECKERBOARD

Horizontal and vertical stripes in a monochromatic scheme make a clear visual impact on this classic cardigan shape. The garment is worked in one piece to the armholes.

■ SIZE
To fit 34[36:38-40]" bust
Figures for larger sizes are given in brackets. Where there is only one set of figures, this applies to all sizes.
See diagram for finished measurements.

■ MATERIALS
Use a lightweight cotton yarn.
8[8:9]oz/200[220:250]g each in contrast A (black) and B (white)
6oz/150g each in contrast C (medium gray) and D (slate gray)
6oz/150g contrast E (light gray)
One each of sizes 4 and 5 circular knitting needle 24" long *or size to obtain correct gauge*
Eight ⅝" buttons
Stitch holders

■ GAUGE
24 sts and 30 rows to 4" over block pat using larger needle
To save time, take time to check gauge.

Note
When working with two colors in a row, weave color not in use loosely across wrong side of work (see page 114). Garment is worked in one piece to armholes.

■ BODY
Using smaller needle and A, cast on 226[246:254] sts and, working back and forth in rows on circular needle, beg rib as foll:
1st rib row (RS) *P2 in A, K2 in B, rep from * ending with P2 in A.
2nd rib row *K2 in A, P2 in B, rep from * ending with K2 in A.
Rep last 2 rows until rib measures 3", ending with a WS row.
Change to larger needle and knit 2 rows in C, dec one st in middle of first row for first and 2nd sizes and inc one st in middle of first row for 3rd size.
225[245:255] sts.
Beg block pat as foll:
Next row (RS) Foll row 3 of chart 1 from right to left, K across row beg and ending as indicated on chart.
Cont foll chart, working first 3rd-7th rows of chart in St st, foll by 2 purl rows in E to form ridge.
Cont in pat in this way (foll chart and always working ridge into 2 stripe rows) without shaping until 63rd row of chart is complete and body measures approx 11½" from beg.

Armhole shaping
Slip 55[60:63] sts from each side of work onto a st holder for fronts and cont on center 115[125:129] sts for back.

■ BACK YOKE
Using A and beg with a RS row, knit 2 rows, binding off 15[18:19] sts at beg of each row. 85[89:91] sts.
Beg with row 66 of chart 2 for yoke, work in pat without shaping foll chart and working ridged stripes as before, until 124th[126th:128th] row of chart is complete and armhole measures approx 8[8¼:8¾]".
Slip sts onto a st holder.

■ RIGHT FRONT YOKE
Slip sts of right front onto larger needle and beg with a RS, knit 2 rows in A, binding off 15[18:19] sts at beg of 2nd row. 40[42:44] sts.
Beg with row 66 of chart 2 for yoke, work in pat as for back yoke without shaping until armhole measures 6¼[6¾:7]", ending with a WS row.

Neck shaping
Cont in pat, binding off 8[9:10] sts at beg of next row (neck edge), then dec one st at neck edge on every row 11 times. 21[22:23] sts.
Cont in pat without shaping until there are the same number of rows as back to shoulder.

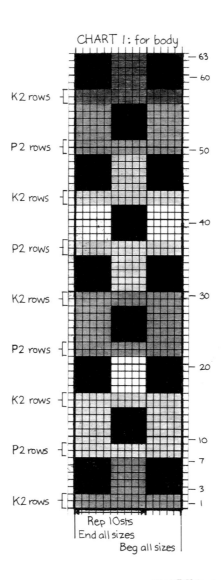

CHART 1: for body

K2 rows
P2 rows
K2 rows
P2 rows
K2 rows
P2 rows
K2 rows
P2 rows
K2 rows

63
60
50
40
30
20
10
7
3
1

Rep 10 sts
End all sizes
Beg all sizes

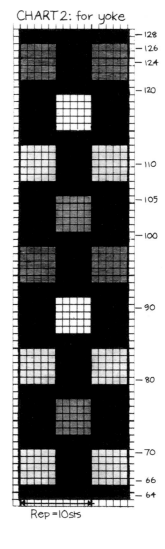

CHART 2: for yoke

128
126
124
120
110
105
100
90
80
70
66
64

Rep = 10 sts

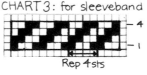

CHART 3: for sleeveband

4
1

Rep 4 sts

Shoulder shaping

** Beg with a WS row and using A, purl 2 rows, knit one row, purl one row. Using E, purl one row. Knit one row.** Rep from ** to ** twice more.
Using A, purl 2 rows. knit one row. Bind off these shoulder sts with sts of right back shoulder by placing WS of back and front tog and binding off first st of back shoulder with first st of front shoulder and so on to form a ridge on the RS.

■ LEFT FRONT YOKE

Work left front yoke as for right front yoke reversing shaping.

■ SLEEVES

Sleeves are worked directly onto body of sweater by picking up sts around armholes.
With RS facing and using larger needle and B, pick up and K115[120:125] sts evenly along armhole edge, omitting bound-off edge at underarm.
Still using B and working back and forth in rows, knit one row.
*** Using A, knit 2 rows, purl one row, knit one row.
Work next 4 rows in St st, foll chart 3 for sleeve band. ***
Rep from *** to *** twice more.
Using A, knit 2 rows, purl one row, knit one row.
Work in pat foll charts, beg with 105th row of chart 2 and working backward to 64th row, then cont on chart 1, beg with 63rd row and working backward to first row, **and at the same time** shape sleeve by dec one st at each end of 6th row once and then every 4th row 24 times. 65[70:75] sts.
Then on last row of pat (row 1 of chart 1) dec 9[14:19] sts evenly across row. 56 sts.
  Change to smaller needle and work in rib as for waistband for 2".
Bind off in A.

■ NECKBAND

With RS facing and using smaller needle and A, beg at right front neck and pick up and K40[41:42] sts along right side of neck, K43[45:47] sts from back neck holder dec one st at center back, pick up and K40[42:44] sts along left side of neck. 122[126:130] sts.
Working back and forth in rows, knit one row in A.

Work in rib as for waistband for 8 rows.
Bind off firmly in A.

■ BUTTONHOLE BAND

With RS facing and using smaller needle and A, pick up and K108[110:112] sts along right front including neckband.
Work 2 rows in rib as for waistband.
Next row Rib 4[4,2], bind off 2 sts, *rib 12[12:13], bind off 2 sts, rep from * to last 4[6:3] sts, rib 2[4:4].
Next row Rib, casting on 2 sts over those bound off in last row.
Work 2 rows in rib. Bind off in A.

■ BUTTON BAND

Work as for buttonhole band, omitting buttonholes.

■ FINISHING

Following manufacturer's directions, block pieces to finished measurements (see page 118).
Join sleeve seam matching pats and sewing first part of top of sleeve to bound-off sts at underarm.
Darn in all loose ends.
Sew on buttons opposite buttonholes.

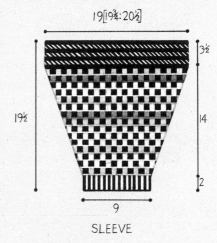

SLEEVE

All measurements are in inches

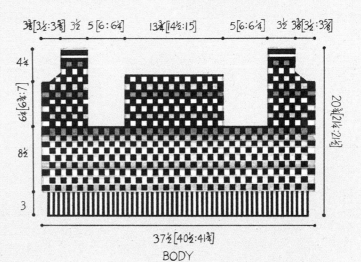

BODY

FIESTA

An off-the-shoulder design ideal for hot sunny days or for evening wear. The scoop neck ruffle in this green flecked top is knitted onto a simple shape and pulled tight to fit with a drawstring.

■ SIZE
To fit 34[36:38-40]" bust
Figures for larger sizes are given in brackets. Where there is only one set of figures, this applies to all sizes. *See diagram for finished measurements.*

■ MATERIALS
11[11:12]oz/300[300:325]g fine cotton yarn
One pair each of sizes 4 and 6 knitting needles *or size to obtain correct gauge*
One size B crochet hook

■ GAUGE
23 sts and 26 rows to 4" over St st using larger needles
To save time, take time to check gauge.

■ BACK AND FRONT (alike)
Using smaller needles, cast on 85 sts and work in rib as foll:
1st rib row (RS) K1, *P1, K1, rep from * to end.
2nd rib row P1, *K1, P1, rep from * to end.
Rep last 2 rows until rib measures 2¼", ending with a WS row.
Change to larger needles and beg with a K row, work in St st shaping sides by inc one st at each end of 5th and every foll 6th row until there are 97[101:109] sts.
Cont without shaping until work measures 18[18½:19]".
Bind off.

■ RUFFLE (Back and front alike)

Using larger needles, cast on 15 sts.

1st and every foll alternate row K2, P to last st, K1.

2nd row (RS) K9, yo, sl 1, K1, psso, yo, K4.

4th row K8, (yo, sl 1, K1, psso) twice, yo, K4.

6th row K7, (yo, sl 1, K1, psso) 3 times, yo, K4.

8th row K6, (yo, sl 1, K1, psso) 4 times, yo, K4.

10th row K5, (yo, sl 1, K1, psso) 5 times, yo, K4.

12th row K4, (yo, sl 1, K1, psso) 6 times, yo, K4.

14th row K5, (yo, sl 1, K1, psso) 6 times, K2tog, K2.

16th row K6, (yo, sl 1, K1, psso) 5 times, K2tog, K2.

18th row K7, (yo, sl 1, K1, psso) 4 times, K2tog, K2.

20th row K8, (yo, sl 1, K1, psso) 3 times, K2tog, K2.

22nd row K9, (yo, sl 1, K1, psso) twice, K2tog, K2.

24th row K10, yo, sl 1, K1, psso, K2tog, K2.

These 24 rows form pat.

Work 11 pat reps more.

Bind off.

■ TOP EDGING

Thread a sewing needle with a length of yarn and make a running stitch along top edge of both ruffles. With RS facing, place along top edge of body, gather evenly to fit body leaving two complete ruffle pats either side for shoulder straps. Tack in place.

With RS facing and using smaller needles, pick up and K147[151:159] sts evenly along top, through ruffle and body, thus attaching ruffle to body.

Work 2 rows in K1, P1 rib.

Eyelet row Rib 2, *rib 2tog, yo, rib 1, rep from * to last 1[2:1] sts, rib to end.

Work 2 rows more in rib.

Bind off.

■ FINISHING

Following manufacturer's directions, block work to finished measurements (see page 118).

Join side seams leaving top 5″ open for armhole and join ruffle seams. Edge armhole with one row of single crochet.

Make a 2yd long braid or twist of yarn; knot approx 1¼″ from each end for tassels.

Thread through eyelets and tie in a bow at front.

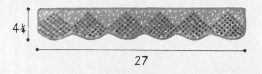

16¾[17¾:19]

15¾[16¼:16¾]

18[18½:19]

2¼

FRONT / BACK

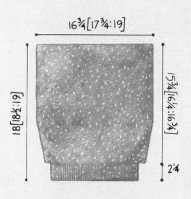

4¼

27

RUFFLE

All measurements are in inches

RIPPLES

This clever juxtaposition of neutral striped panels in both pullover and jacket looks complicated to knit, but it is not. Each section is knitted onto the previous section, and there is the minimum of finishing. A variation on the pattern, turning it into a jacket, is given on page 66.

◼ SIZE

One size to fit up to 38" bust
See diagram for finished measurements.

◼ MATERIALS

44oz/1200g medium weight cotton yarn for pullover
4oz/100g of contrast yarn for jacket version
One pair of size 8 knitting needles *or size to obtain correct gauge*

◼ GAUGE

16 sts and 23 rows to 4" over pat
To save time, take time to check gauge.

◼ STITCHES

1st and 3rd rows P.
2nd and 4th rows K.
5th and 7th rows K.
6th and 8th rows P.
These 8 rows form pat and are worked throughout.

Note

For the jacket version, work in 4 rows of contrast yarn at random on each section or following the photograph. Where chart details dec 2 sts at end of row, work 3 sts tog.

◼ BACK

(Worked in 4 sections)
Section One
Cast on 50 sts and work in pat foll shaping from chart 1 for 102 rows.
Fasten off.
Section Two
With RS facing, pick up and K87 sts evenly along shaped edge of section one (A) and work in pat foll shaping from chart 2 for 96 rows, placing marker at beg of row 48.
Fasten off.
Section Three
With RS facing, pick up and K48 sts evenly along edge of section two from center marker to left hand edge (B) and work in pat foll shaping from chart 3 for 69 rows.
Bind off rem 2 sts.
Section Four
With RS facing, pick up and K42 sts evenly along inside edge row ends of section three (C) and work in pat foll shaping from chart 4 for 86 rows.
Bind off rem 3 sts.

◼ FRONT

(Worked in 4 sections)
Work first three sections as for back.
Section Four
Cast on one st and work in pat foll shaping from chart 4 for 86 rows.
Bind off rem 3 sts.

◼ SLEEVES

(Worked in 2 sections)
Section One
Cast on 58 sts and work in pat foll shapings from chart 5 for 87 rows.
Bind off rem 24 sts.
Section Two
With RS facing, pick up and K61 sts evenly along straight edge of section one (D) and work in pat foll shaping from chart 6 for 69 rows.
Fasten off.

◼ WAISTBANDS (2 alike)

With RS facing, pick up and K60 sts evenly along bottom edge.
Work in pat for 4 rows.
Bind off loosely.

◼ CUFFS (2 alike)

With RS facing, pick up and K32 sts evenly along bottom sleeve edge.
Work in pat for 4 rows.
Bind off loosely.

◼ COLLAR

Cast on 104 sts and work in pat for 32 rows.
Bind off loosely.

■ FINISHING

Following manufacturer's directions, block pieces to finished measurements (see page 118).
Join section four to section two on front and back.
Join shoulder seams.
Sew sleeves to back and front.
Join side and sleeve seams.
Join short ends of collar and sew collar to neck edge.

JACKET

■ BACK

Work as for back of pullover.

■ SLEEVES

Work as for sleeves of pullover.

■ LEFT FRONT (Worked in 4 sections)

Section One
Cast on 50 sts and work in pat foll shaping from chart 7 for 102 rows.
Fasten off.

Section Two
With RS facing, pick up and K87 sts evenly along shaped edge of section one (A) and work in pat foll shaping from chart 8 for 60 rows, placing marker at beg of row 48.
Fasten off.

Section Three
With RS facing, pick up and K48 sts evenly along edge of section two from center marker to left-hand edge (B) and work in pat foll shaping from chart 9 for 69 rows.
Fasten off.

Section Four
With RS facing, pick up and K42 sts evenly along inside edge of row ends of section three (C) and work in pat foll shaping from chart 10 for 41 rows.
Fasten off.

■ RIGHT FRONT (Worked in 3 sections)

Section One
Cast on one st and work in pat foll shaping from chart 11 for 102 rows.
Fasten off.

Section Two
With RS facing, pick up and K51 sts evenly along shaped edge of section one (A) and work in pat foll shaping from chart 12 for 96 rows.
Fasten off.

Section Three
Cast on 2 sts and work in pat foll shaping from chart 13 for 55 rows.
52 sts.
56th row (WS) Pat 14 sts, turn and leave rem sts on a spare needle. Work rem rows on left-hand side of chart.
Fasten off.
With WS facing, rejoin yarn to rem 38 sts, work 3sts tog, pat to end.
Work rem rows of right hand side of chart.
Fasten off.

■ BACK WAISTBAND

With RS facing, pick up and K60 sts evenly along bottom edge of back.
Work in pat for 12 rows.
Bind off.

■ FRONT WAISTBANDS (2 alike)

With RS facing, pick up and K30 sts evenly along bottom edge of both front sections.
Work in pat for 12 rows.
Bind off.

■ FINISHING

Following manufacturer's directions, block pieces to finished measurements (see page 118).
Sew sleeves to back and fronts.
Join side and sleeve seams.

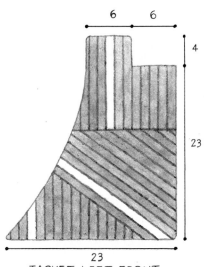

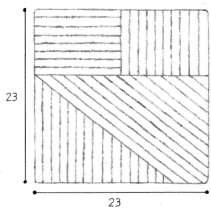

23
23

PULLOVER FRONT / BACK
JACKET BACK

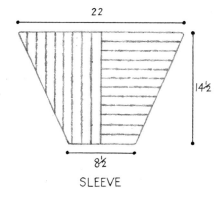

22
14½
8½

SLEEVE

All measurements are in inches

6 6
4
23
23

JACKET LEFT FRONT

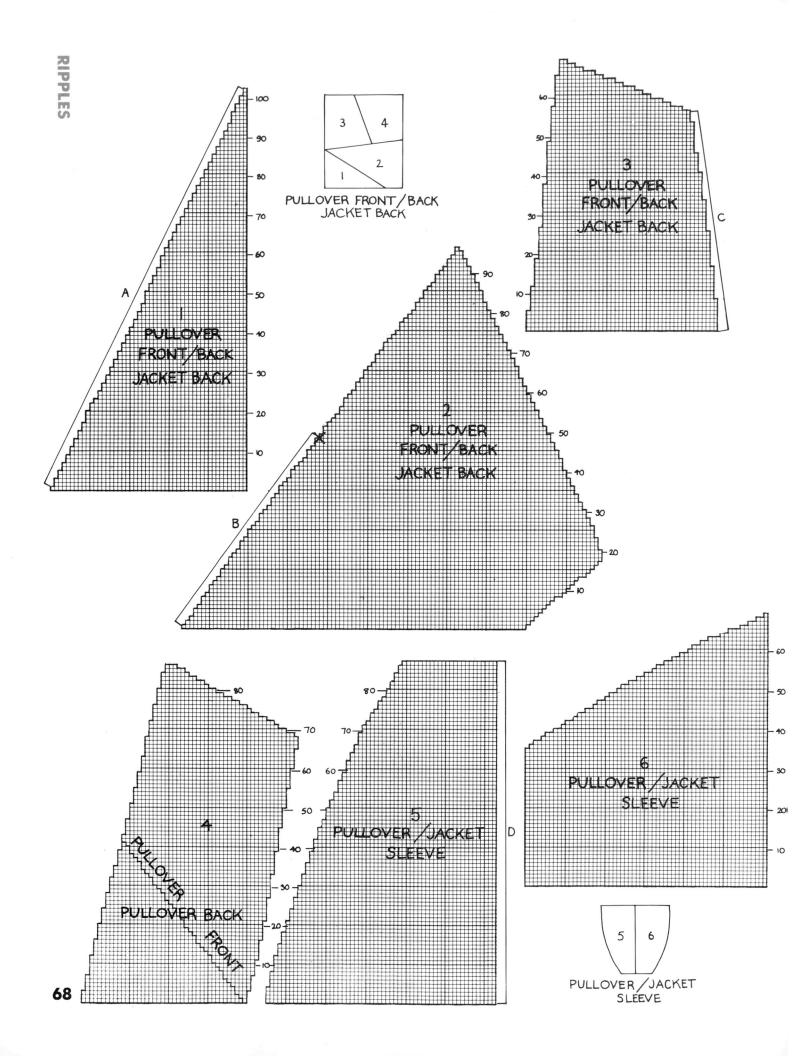

A

PULLOVER
FRONT/BACK
JACKET BACK

3
4
1
2

PULLOVER FRONT/BACK
JACKET BACK

3
PULLOVER
FRONT/BACK
JACKET BACK

C

B

X

2
PULLOVER
FRONT/BACK
JACKET BACK

4
PULLOVER
PULLOVER BACK
FRONT

5
PULLOVER/JACKET
SLEEVE

D

6
PULLOVER/JACKET
SLEEVE

5   6

PULLOVER/JACKET
SLEEVE

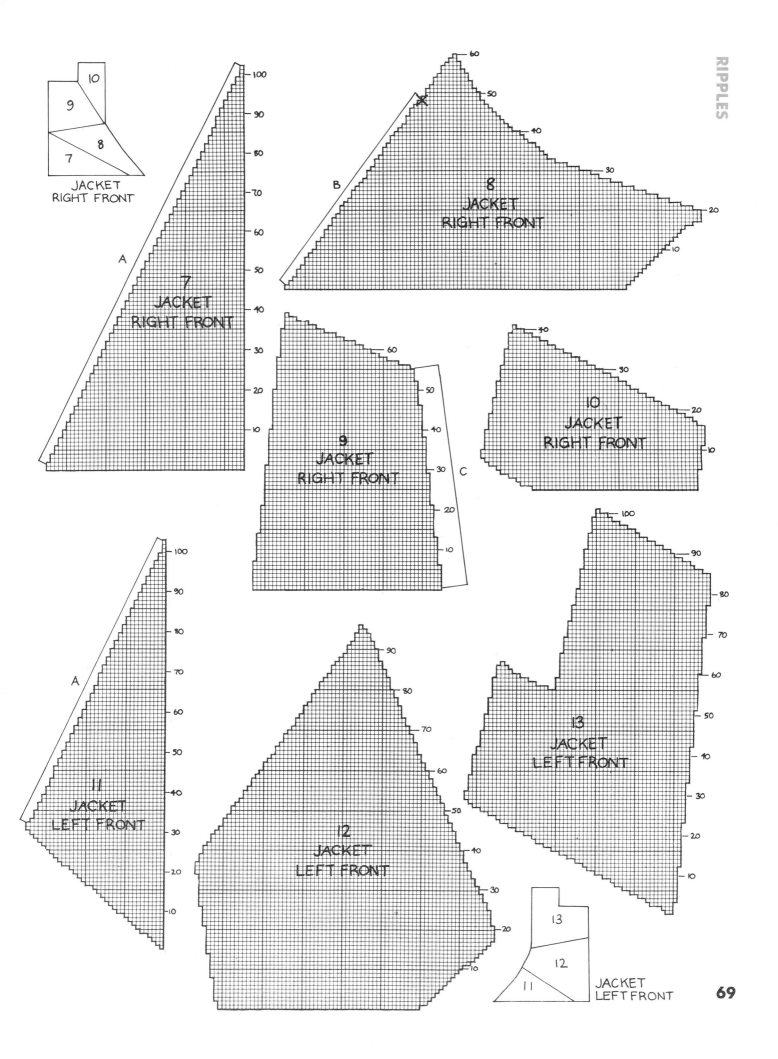

10

9

7   8

JACKET
RIGHT FRONT

A

7
JACKET
RIGHT FRONT

B

8
JACKET
RIGHT FRONT

9
JACKET
RIGHT FRONT

C

10
JACKET
RIGHT FRONT

A

11
JACKET
LEFT FRONT

12
JACKET
LEFT FRONT

13
JACKET
LEFT FRONT

13

12

11

JACKET
LEFT FRONT

STRIPE SURPRISE

With its sharply contrasting horizontal and vertical stripes, this T-shaped sweater has a lot of impact. You can experiment with stripes within this pattern to create your own unique combination (see page 73).

■ SIZE

To fit 32-34[36:38]" bust
Figures for larger sizes are given in brackets. Where there is only one set of figures, this applies to all sizes. *See diagram for finished measurements.*

■ MATERIALS

Use a medium weight cotton yarn.
16[16:18]oz/450[450:500]g main color A (black)
11[11:13]oz/300[300:350]g first contrast B (lilac)
4oz/100g 2nd contrast C (turquoise)
One pair of size 7 knitting needles
One 16"-long size 7 circular knitting needle
One 24"-long size 7 circular knitting needle *or size to obtain correct gauge*
Stitch holders

■ GAUGE

20 sts and 28 rows to 4" over St st
To save time, take time to check gauge.

Note

Lower edge of sleeves and neckband are worked in St st and are meant to roll to RS.
Lower edge of back and front are worked in rev St st and are meant to roll to WS.

■ BACK

Using straight needles and A, cast on 82[86:90] sts and beg with a K row, work in St st and stripe pat as foll:
* 20 rows using A.
10 rows using B. *
Rep from * to * without shaping until back measures 19[19¼:19¾]", ending with a WS row.

Neck shaping

Next row (RS) K25[26:27] sts, turn and leave rem sts on a spare needle.
Work 5 rows without shaping on these 25[26:27] sts.
Bind off.
With RS facing, slip center 32[34:36] sts onto st holder for back neck.
Rejoin yarn to rem sts and work to match first side.

■ FRONT

Work as for back until front measures 17[17¼:17¾]", ending with a WS row.

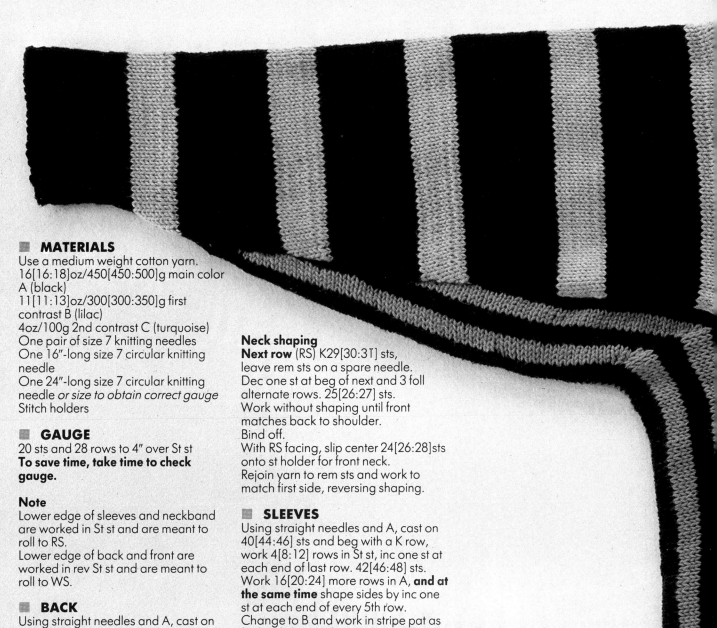

Neck shaping

Next row (RS) K29[30:31] sts, leave rem sts on a spare needle.
Dec one st at beg of next and 3 foll alternate rows. 25[26:27] sts.
Work without shaping until front matches back to shoulder.
Bind off.
With RS facing, slip center 24[26:28]sts onto st holder for front neck.
Rejoin yarn to rem sts and work to match first side, reversing shaping.

■ SLEEVES

Using straight needles and A, cast on 40[44:46] sts and beg with a K row, work 4[8:12] rows in St st, inc one st at each end of last row. 42[46:48] sts.
Work 16[20:24] more rows in A, **and at the same time** shape sides by inc one st at each end of every 5th row.
Change to B and work in stripe pat as for back, beg with 10 rows B and cont to inc one st at each end of every 5th row until there are 84[88:92] sts.
Cont without shaping until sleeve measures approx 21¼[21½:22]", ending with a stripe of 10 rows in B.
Bind off.

■ UNDERARM INSETS (4 pieces)

Each underarm inset is made in 2 pieces – front and back.

Right front and left back inset

(Make 2)
Using straight needles and A, cast on 80 sts.
1st row P to end.
2nd row Cast on 5 sts, K to end.
3rd row P50, (P2tog) twice, P to end.
4th row As 2nd row.
Using C, rep last 2 rows twice.
9th row Using A, as 3rd row.
Rows 2-9 form pat.

Cont in pat until 23 rows have been completed, ending with 3 rows in C. Bind off.

Right back and left front inset
(Make 2)
Using straight needles and A, cast on 80 sts.
1st row K to end.
2nd row Cast on 5 sts, P to end.
3rd row K50, (K2tog) twice, K to end.

4th row As 2nd row.
Using C, rep last 2 rows twice.
9th row Using A, as 3rd row.
Rows 2–9 form pat.
Cont in pat until 23 rows have been completed, ending with 3 rows in C. Bind off.

█ NECKBAND
Join shoulder seams.
With RS facing and using shorter

circular needle and A, K across 32[34:36] sts of center back from st holder, pick up and K18 sts evenly along left side of neck to center front, K across 24[26:28] sts of center front from st holder, pick up and K18 sts evenly along right side of neck. 92[96:100] sts.
Knit 15 rounds (St st) without shaping. Bind off firmly to ensure that edge rolls to RS.

FINISHING

Following manufacturer's directions, block pieces to finished measurements (see page 118).
Mark position of sleeves 8¼[8½:9]" from shoulder seams on back and front.
Sew sleeves to back and front between markers.
Join right front and right back insets.
Join left front and left back insets.
Sew insets to back and front, matching straight end of inset with lower edge of back and front with shaped end approx 3[3¼:4]" from lower sleeve edge.

LOWER EDGING

With RS facing, using larger circular needle and A, pick up and K204[212:220] sts evenly around lower edge of back and front.
Purl 6 rounds (rev St st) without shaping.
Bind off firmly to insure that edge rolls to WS.

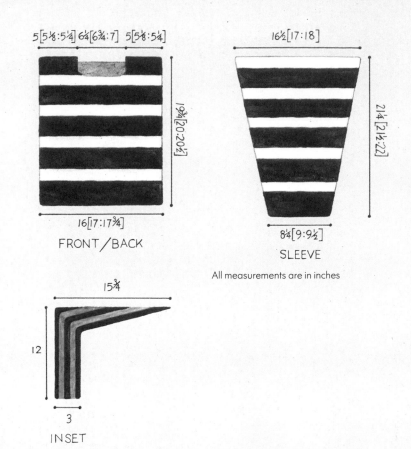

5[5⅛:5¼] 6¼[6¾:7] 5[5⅛:5¼]

19¾[20:20½]

16[17:17¾]

FRONT/BACK

16½[17:18]

21¼[21½:22]

8¼[9:9½]

SLEEVE

All measurements are in inches

15¾

12

3

INSET

SIMPLE STRIPE VARIATIONS

The simple but effective transposition of stripes on this design can be used as the basis for any number of different garments. The stripes need not be a consistently standard width; they can be interspersed with a single row of color as a highlight or follow the colors of the rainbow. By using the same color scheme horizontally across the back and front and vertically on the insets you can achieve remarkable visual effects. The samples shown here are in soft mellow tones of pink, green, gray, white and black. To help design your own, knit the striped samples first and play around with them so that you can envision the end result more clearly.

The patterns for these stripe variations can be incorporated into the master pattern by replacing the stripes with your own width of stripe and number of colors, while maintaining the stockinette stitch and shaping throughout. Remember to change the color on a right side row.

1 2 rows of black between every 2 rows of the other 4 colors – pink, green, white and gray in this sample.
2 10 rows of each color – gray, pink, green and white – separated by 2 rows of black.
3 Maintaining the 2 rows of black between every color change, work 4 stripes of each color, each stripe 2 rows deep.
4 10 rows gray and 2 rows black.

REGATTA

With its pattern of narrow stripes and classic shaping this crew neck sweater has a twenties boating air.

■ SIZE
To fit 34[36:38]" bust
Figures for larger sizes are given in brackets. Where there is only one set of figures, this applies to all sizes.
See diagram for finished measurements.

■ MATERIALS
Use a medium weight cotton yarn.
16[16:17]oz/450[450:475]g main color A (blue)
7oz/200g contrast B (maroon)
One pair each of sizes 3, 6 and 8 knitting needles *or size to obtain correct gauge*

■ GAUGE
16 sts and 21 rows to 4" over St st using largest needles
To save time, take time to check gauge.

Note
Read chart from right to left for RS knit rows and left to right for WS purl rows. Unless stated St st is used throughout. Sleeves are knitted sideways.

■ FRONT
** Using medium size needles and A, cast on 69[73:77] sts and work 4[6:8] rows in K1, P1 rib.
Change to largest needles and purl one row.
Beg with row 1 of chart and a knit row, work from chart shaping sides by inc one st at each end of 24th, 47th and 70th rows. 75[79:83] sts.
Cont from chart without shaping until end of row 79[77:75].

Armhole shaping
Bind off 3 sts at beg of next 2 rows. 69[73:77] sts.
Dec one st at each end of next and foll 3 alternate rows. 61[65:69] sts. **
Cont from chart without shaping until end of row 126.

Neck shaping
Next row P23[25:27] sts, bind off center 15 sts, P to end.
Work one row.
Bind off 3 sts at beg of next and foll alternate row. 17[19:21] sts.
Work one row.
Dec one st at neck edge on next and foll alternate row. 15[17:19] sts.
Work 2 rows without shaping.
Bind off.

With RS facing, rejoin yarn to rem sts and work to match first side, reversing shaping.

■ BACK
Work as for front from ** to **.
Cont without shaping omitting "V"-shaped striped pat at neck until end of row 134.

Neck shaping
Next row K15[17:19], turn, P to end.
Bind off.
With RS facing, rejoin yarn to rem sts, bind off center 31 sts, K to end.
Purl one row.
Bind off.

■ LEFT SLEEVE
Using largest needles and A, cast on 6 sts and beg with a K row, work 2 rows in St st without shaping.
Cast on 5 sts at beg of next and foll alternate row. 16 sts.
*** Cast on 2 sts at beg of next row.
Cast on 5 sts at beg of next row.***
Rep last 2 rows twice. 37 sts.
Cast on 3 sts at beg of next row.
Cast on 5 sts at beg of next row.
Rep last 2 rows once. 53 sts.
Rep from *** to *** twice. 67 sts.
Inc one st at beg of next row.
Cast on 5 sts at beg of next row.
Rep last 2 rows once. 79 sts.
Inc one st at beg of next and 2 foll alternate rows. 82 sts.
Cont from chart without shaping to end of row 60[61:63].
Dec one st at beg of next and 2 foll alternate rows. 79 sts.
Bind off 5 sts at beg of next row.
Dec one st at beg of next row.
Rep last 2 rows once. 67 sts.
**** Bind off 5 sts at beg of next row.
Bind off 2 sts at beg of next row. ****
Rep last 2 rows once. 53 sts.
Bind off 5 sts at beg of next row.
Bind off 3 sts at beg of next row.
Rep last 2 rows once. 37 sts.
Rep from **** to **** 3 times. 16 sts.
Bind off 5 sts at beg of next and foll alternate row. 6 sts.
Work 2 rows without shaping.
Bind off.

■ RIGHT SLEEVE
Work as for left sleeve, omitting stripes and working 2nd half of sleeve in B.

■ FRONT NECKBAND
With RS facing and using smallest needles and A, pick up and K59 sts evenly around front neck.
Work 4 rows in P1, K1 rib.
Bind off evenly in rib.

■ BACK NECKBAND
With RS facing and using smallest needles and A, pick up and K47 sts

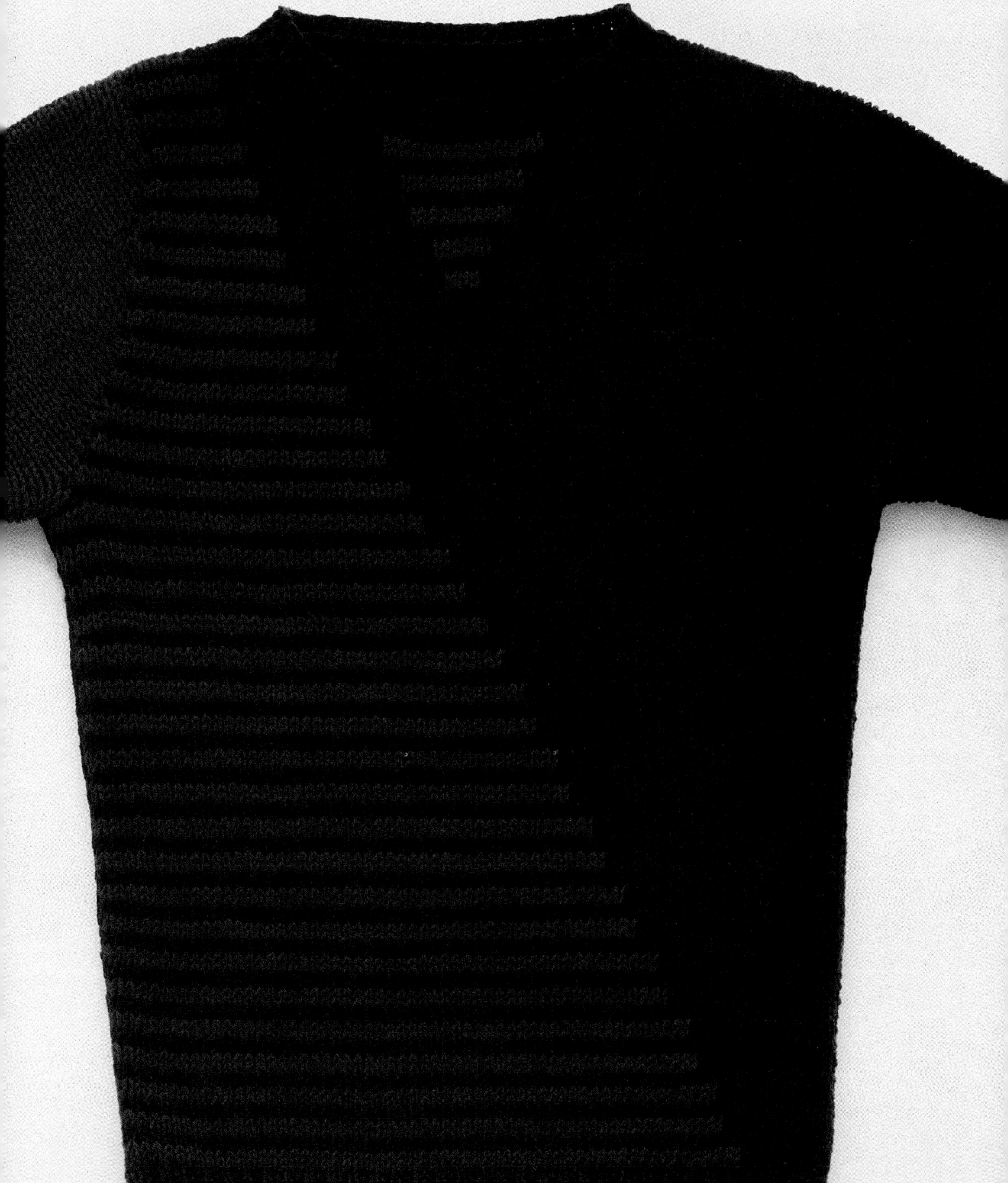

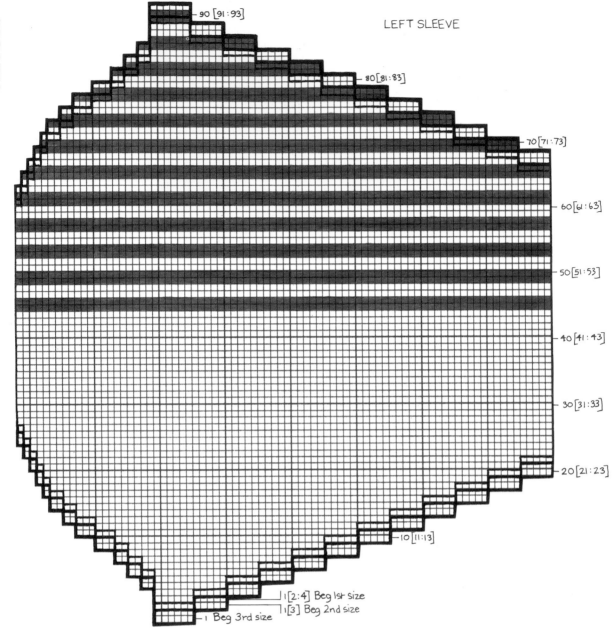

LEFT SLEEVE

90 [91:93]

80 [81:83]

70 [71:73]

60 [61:63]

50 [51:53]

40 [41:43]

30 [31:33]

20 [21:23]

10 [11:13]

1 [2:4] Beg 1st size
1 [3] Beg 2nd size
1 Beg 3rd size

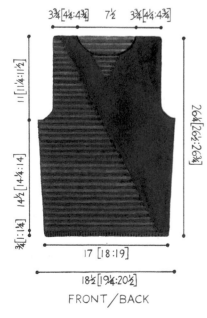

3¾ [4¼:4¾]   7½   3¾ [4¼:4¾]

11 [11¼:11½]

26½ [26½:26¾]

14½ [14¼:14]

¾ [1:1¼]

17 [18:19]

18½ [19¼:20½]

FRONT / BACK

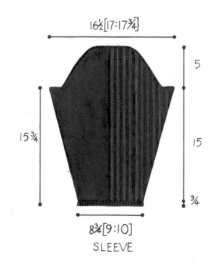

16½ [17:17¾]

5

15¾

15

8¾ [9:10]

¾

SLEEVE

evenly around back neck.
Work 4 rows in P1, K1 rib.
Bind off evenly in rib.

CUFFS
With RS facing and using smallest
needles and A, pick up and K41[43:45]
sts evenly along each cuff.
Work 5 rows in P1, K1 rib.
Bind off.

FINISHING
Following manufacturer's directions,
block pieces to finished measurements
(see page 118).
Join shoulders and neckbands.
Join side and sleeve seams.
Sew in sleeves matching stripes at left
sleeve cap to stripes on back.

All measurements are in inches

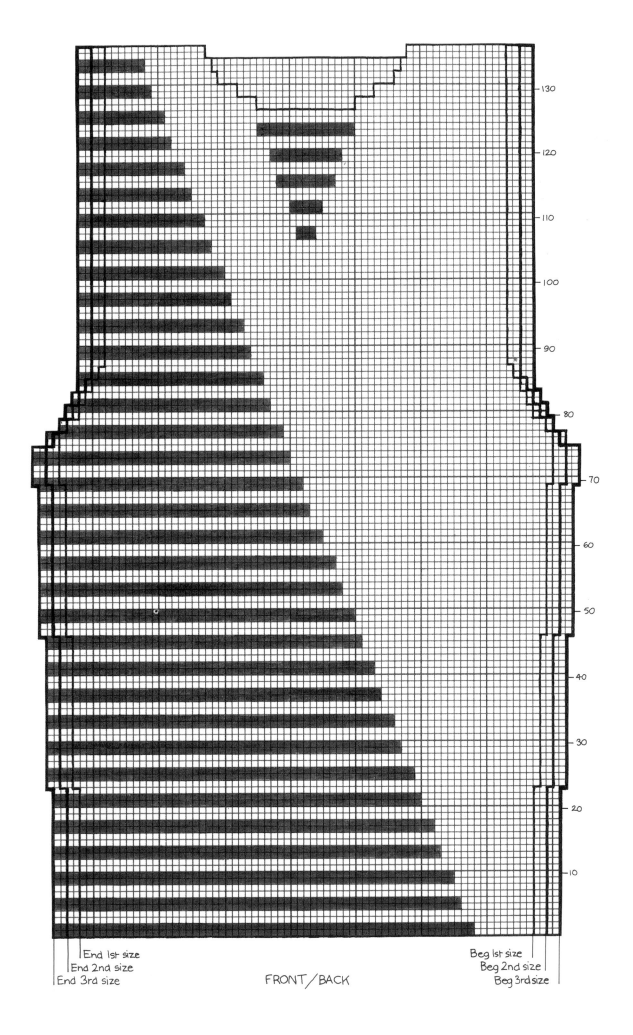

End 1st size
End 2nd size
End 3rd size

FRONT/BACK

Beg 1st size
Beg 2nd size
Beg 3rd size

130

120

110

100

90

80

70

60

50

40

30

20

10

LACE UP

A very simple shape, which can be
knitted to any length, and an
interesting lace stitch provide the basis
for a number of design variations.
Experiment by threading other
materials through the lace.

■ SIZE
One size to fit up to 38" bust
*See diagram for finished
measurements.*

■ MATERIALS
Use a lightweight cotton yarn.
10oz/280g short top
18oz/500g dress version
One pair of size 8 knitting needles *or
size to obtain correct gauge*

■ GAUGE
17 sts and 27 rows to 4" over pat using
size 8 needles
**To save time, take time to check
gauge.**

■ BACK AND FRONT (alike)

Cast on 86 sts and work in pat as foll:

1st row K3, *yo, K3, sl 1, K2tog, psso, K3, yo, K1, rep from * to last 3 sts, K3.

2nd, 4th and 6th rows P.

3rd row K3, *K1, yo, K2, sl 1, K2tog, psso, K2, yo, K2, rep from * to last 3 sts, K3.

5th row K3, *K2, yo, K1, sl 1, K2tog, psso, K1, yo, K3, rep from * to last 3 sts, K3.

7th row K3, *K3, yo, sl 1, K2tog, psso, yo, K4, rep from * to last 3 sts, K3.

8th row P3, K to last 3 sts, P3.

Rep last 8 rows 15 times more.

Next row K.

Next row P.

Bind off.

■ FINISHING

Thread colors through the loop formed by psso in the lace pattern and secure at top and bottom of garment on WS.

Join shoulder seams for 4", leaving 12" open for neck.

Join side seams, leaving 10" open for armhole.

Following manufacturer's directions, block sweater to finished measurements (see page 118).

DRESS VERSION

To extend lace pat for dress, cont in pat until you reach the desired length.

Next row (RS) K.

Next row P.

Bind off.

■ FINISHING

As for short version.

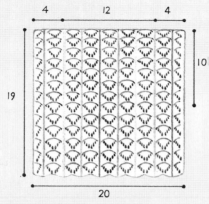

FRONT / BACK

All measurements are in inches

CHANGING THREADS

By using different yarns and threading them through the lace pattern in different ways, you can create a variety of effects with this simple top.

1 Find the ridge of purl stitches that forms the tops of the lace V and run the yarn through the bottom loop of the stitch and over to form an overstitch across the garment. To make tassels, take three pieces of yarn, each 4" long, and thread them through the two holes at the bottom of the lace V. Tie them lightly in a double knot and cut the ends ¾" from the knot.

2 Cut lengths of fabric into ¾"-wide strips. Press in half lengthwise and thread across the garment through all the holes of the lace V.

3 Use two strands of yarn and take them across the garment through all the holes of the lace V.

4 In this neutral-colored version, the yarns have been threaded double in the same way as the threads on the main design.

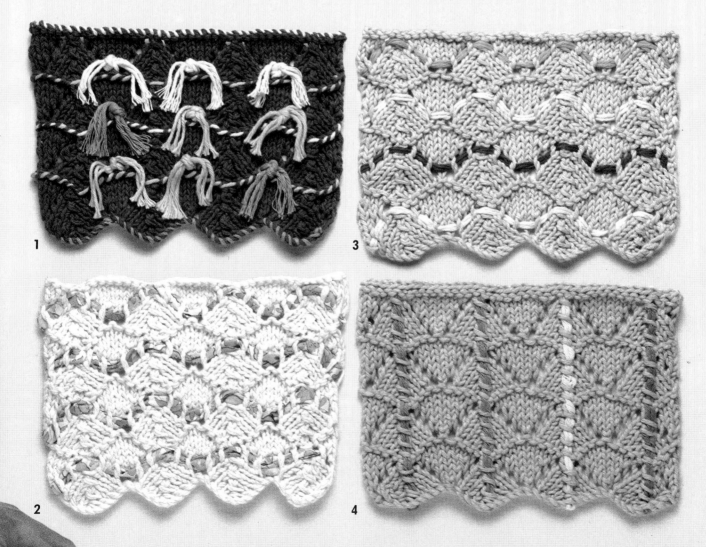

TIGER TAILS

Tails of harmonizing colors wind across this batwing sweater, producing an exciting contrast with the background.

■ SIZE

One size to fit up to 36" bust
See diagram for finished measurements.

■ MATERIALS

Use a lightweight cotton slub yarn for the main color and lightweight and medium weight cotton yarns for the contrast in either bouclé, slub, smooth or mercerized.

18oz/500g main color A (brown)
2oz/50g each in 10 harmonizing colors B,C,D,E,F,G,H,J,L,N (blue)
One size B crochet hook
One pair each of size 5 and 7 knitting needles (or circular knitting needle if preferred) *or size to obtain correct gauge*
Bobbins

■ GAUGE

18 sts and 24 rows to 4" over St st using larger needles
To save time, take time to check gauge.

Note

The main color (A) is used double throughout; the other yarns are used in combination or singly.
Do not carry colors across; use separate bobbins of yarn for each color section. When changing colors, pick up new color from under dropped color to prevent holes (see page 114).
Read chart from right to left for RS knit rows and left to right for WS purl rows.
Unless stated St st is used throughout.
This garment is worked in one piece.

■ BODY

Back

Using smaller needles and F, cast on 81 sts, change to A and work in rib as foll:
1st rib row (RS) K1, *P1, K1, rep from * to end.
2nd rib row P1, *K1, P1, rep from * to end.
Rep last 2 rows 6 times.
15th rib row As first rib row.
Inc row Rib 2, (M1, rib 2) 39 times, rib 1. 120 sts.

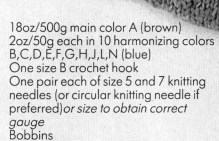

Change to larger needles, and beg with a K row, work in St st from row 1 of chart for 34 rows.

Sleeve shaping

Cont in pat, cast on 5 sts at beg of next 20 rows. 220 sts.
Cont without shaping to end of row 102.

Neck shaping

Next row Pat 97 sts, turn and leave rem sts on a spare needle.
**Bind off 6 sts at beg of next row and 4 sts on foll alternate row. Work one row. Inc one st at beg of next and foll alternate row.
Work one row.
Inc 2 sts at beg of next and foll alternate row.
Work one row.
Inc 3 sts at beg of next row.
Work one row.
Inc 4 sts at beg of next row.**

Work one row. 100 sts.
Leave these sts on a spare needle.
With RS facing, rejoin yarn A to rem sts, bind off 26 sts and pat to end.
P one row.
Work from ** to ** as for first side, ending with a K row.
Next row P to end, cast on 20 sts, P across sts of first side from spare needle. 220 sts.
Cont without shaping down front until end of row 160.

Sleeve shaping
Bind off 5 sts at beg of next 20 rows.
120 sts.
Cont without shaping to end of chart.
Change to smaller needles and A only.
Next row K1, P1, (K2tog, P1) to last st,
K1. 81 sts.
Beg with 2nd row, work in rib as for
back for 15 rows.
Change to F and work one row in rib.
Bind off in F.

◼ CUFFS

Using smaller needles and A, pick up
53 sts evenly along end of sleeve and
work in P1, K1 rib for 15 rows.
Change to F and work one row in rib.
Bind off in F.

◼ NECK EDGING

Using A singly, work 2 rows of single
crochet evenly around neck edge.

◼ FINISHING

Following manufacturer's directions,
block work to finished measurements
(see page 118).
Join side and underarm seams.

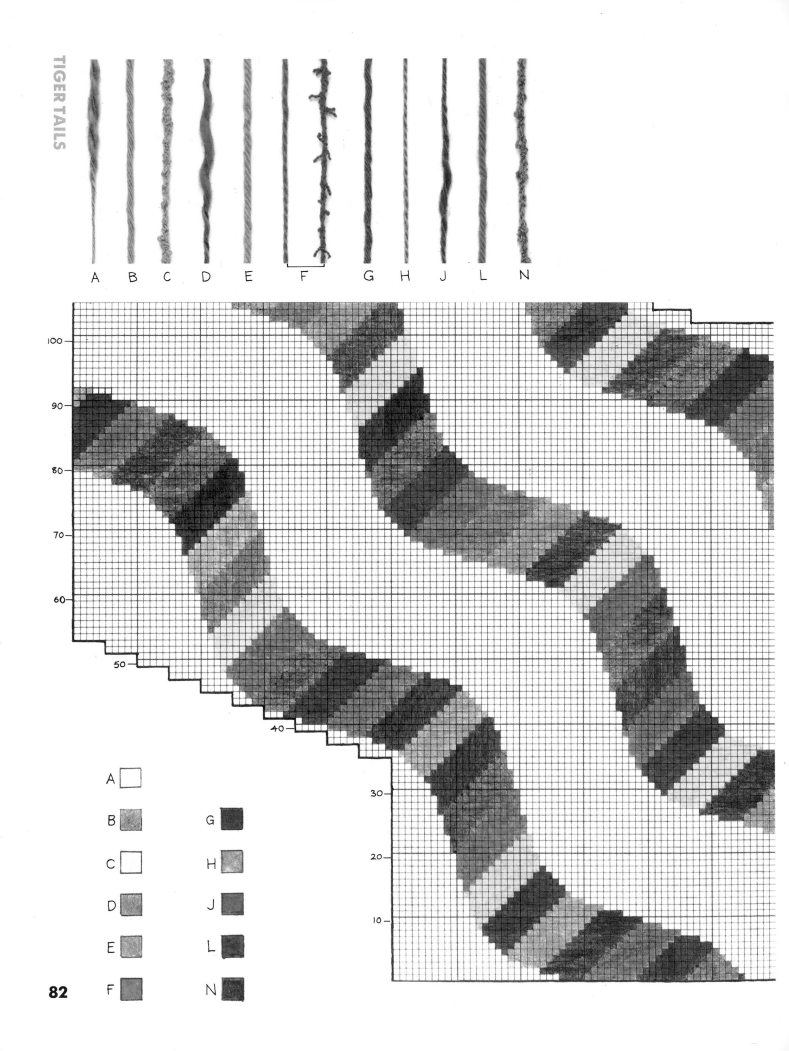

A B C D E F G H J L N

A
B   G
C   H
D   J
E   L

F   N

Chart continues on pages 84 and 85

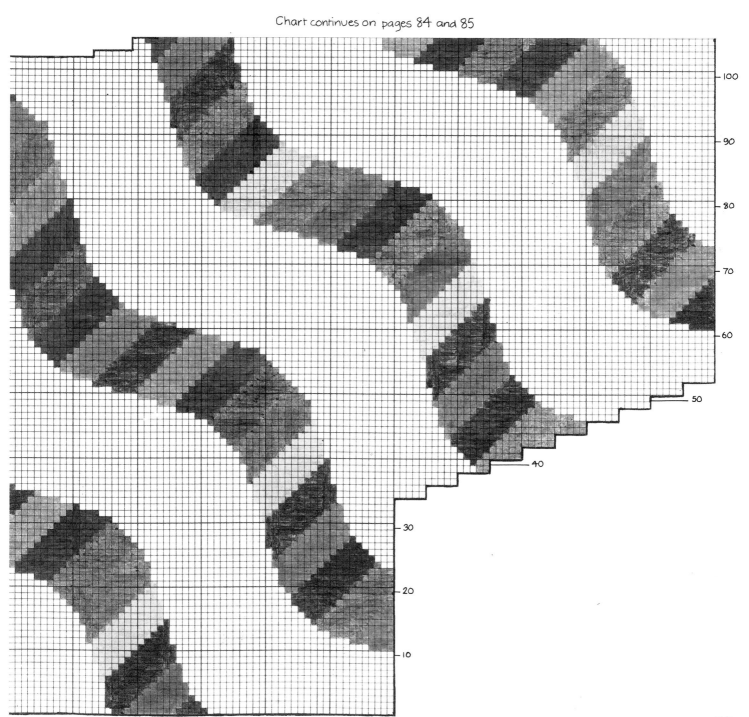

100

90

80

70

60

50

40

30

20

10

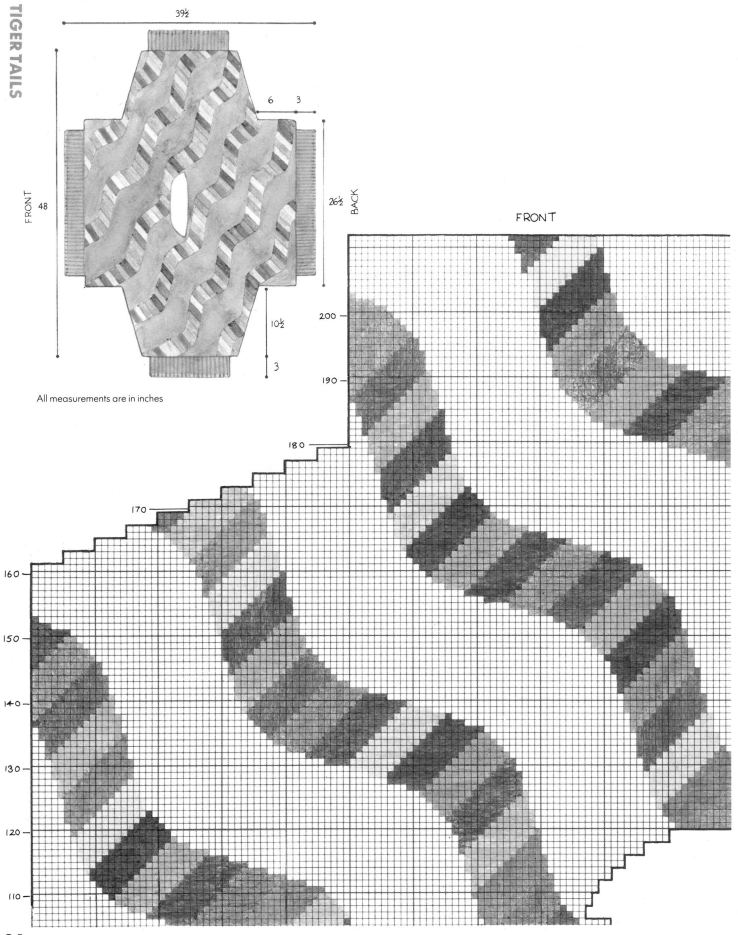

39½

6 3

FRONT 48

26½ BACK

10½

3

All measurements are in inches

FRONT

200

190

180

170

160

150

140

130

120

110

Chart continued from page 82

FRONT

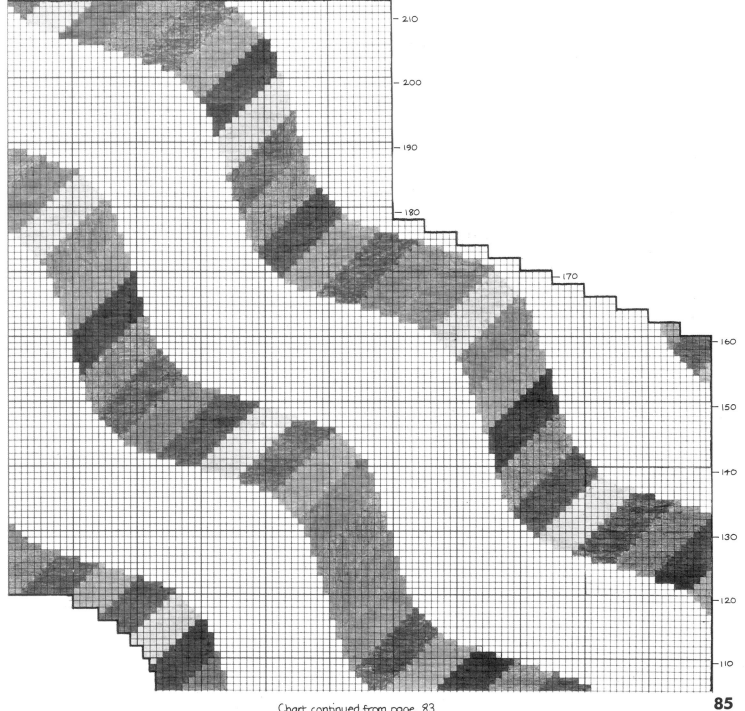

Chart continued from page 83

SWEET CHESTNUT

A variety of lacy stitches have been used in this short-sleeved top. A pastel color would emphasize the stitch pattern.

■ SIZE

One size to fit up to 40" bust
See diagram for finished measurements.

■ MATERIALS

9oz/250g lightweight cotton yarn
One pair each of size 4 and 6 knitting needles *or size to obtain correct gauge*
Three ⅝"-¾" buttons
Ring markers

■ GAUGE

24 sts and 30 rows to 4" over pat using larger needles
To save time, take time to check gauge.

■ BACK

Using smaller needles, cast on 125 sts and work in rib as foll:
1st rib row (RS) K1, *P1, K1, rep from * to end.
2nd rib row P1, *K1, P1, rep from * to end.

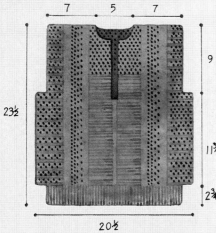

7 5 7

9

23½

11¾

2¾

20½

FRONT/BACK

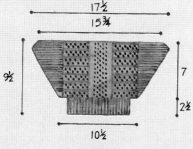

17½

15¾

9½

7

2½

10½

SLEEVE

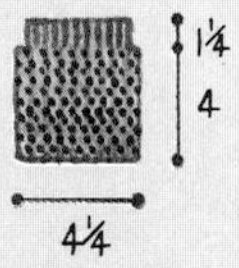

1¼

4

4¼

POCKET

All measurements are in inches

86

Rep last 2 rows until rib measures 2¾", ending with a 2nd row, inc one st in last row. 126 sts.
Change to larger needles and work in pat as foll:
1st row K4, P1, (K1, yo, K2tog) 5 times, K1, P1, K2, P1, K12, yo, K2tog, K2, P1, K2, (P18, K2) twice, P1, K12, yo, K2tog, (K2, P1) twice, (K1, yo, K2tog) 5 times, K1, P1, K4.
2nd row P2, (P2, K1, P16, K1) twice, P42, (K1, P16, K1, P2) twice, P2.
3rd row K4, P1, K2, (K1, yo, K2tog) 4 times, (K2, P1) twice, K10, yo, K2tog, K4, P1, K2, (P18, K2) twice, P1, K10, yo, K2tog, K4, P1, K2, P1, K2, (K1, yo, K2tog) 4 times, K2, P1, K4.
4th row As 2nd row.
5th row K4, P1, K16, P1, K2, P1, K8, (yo, K2tog, K2) twice, P1, K2, (P18, K2) twice, P1, K8, (yo, K2tog, K2) twice, P1, K2, P1, K16, P1, K4.
6th row P4, K18, P2, K1, P16, K1, P2, (K18, P2) twice, K1, P16, K1, P2, K18, P4.
7th row K4, P1, K16, P1, K2, P1, K6, (yo, K2tog, K2) twice, K2, P1, K2, (P18, K2) twice, P1, K6, (yo, K2tog, K2) twice, (K2, P1) twice, K16, P1, K4.
8th row As 2nd row.
These 8 rows form pat.
Cont without shaping until back measures 14½", ending with a WS row.

Shape armholes

Bind off 6 sts at beg of next 2 rows. 114 sts.
Cont without shaping *working 4 sts in St st at each end of row* until armhole measures 5", ending with a WS row. Using ring markers, mark positions of 16 central sts of each of 2 central panels.
Keeping to pat as set on all sts but the 2 sets of 16 sts, work mesh st over these 2 sets of 16 sts on next 4 rows as foll:
1st row (RS) (K1, yo, K2tog) 5 times, K1.
2nd row P.
3rd row K2, (K1, yo, K2tog) 4 times, K2.
4th row P.
These 4 rows form mesh pat.
Cont in pat as set until armhole measures 8¼".

Neck shaping

Next row Pat 45 sts, turn and leave rem sts on a spare needle.
Dec one st at neck edge on next and 2 foll alternate rows. 42 sts.
Bind off.
With RS facing, rejoin yarn to rem sts. Bind off center 24 sts, work to match first side, reversing shaping.

■ FRONT

Work as for back until front measures 13".

Divide front

Next row Pat 63 sts, turn and leave rem sts on a spare needle.
Cont on these 63 sts without shaping *keeping 3 sts at neck edge in St st,* until front measures same as back to armhole, ending with a WS row.

Shape armhole

Bind off 6 sts at beg of next row. 57 sts.
Cont without shaping until armhole measures 2", ending with a WS row. Now working central panel of 16 sts in mesh st, cont without shaping until front measures 17 rows less than back to shoulder.

Neck shaping

Bind off 11 sts at beg of next row.
Work 3 rows.
Dec one st (3 sts in from edge) on next and foll 4th row 3 times. 42 sts.
Bind off.
With RS facing, rejoin yarn to rem sts and work to match first side, reversing shapings.

■ SLEEVES

Using smaller needles, cast on 65 sts and work in rib as for back for 2½", inc one st in last row. 66 sts.
Change to larger needles and work in 8 row pat as foll, **and at the same time** shape sides by inc one st at each end (4 sts in from edge) of 3rd and every foll alternate row until there are 107 sts, working inc sts in mesh pat as for central panels on back and front.
1st row K4, P1, *(K1, yo, K2tog) 5 times, K1, P1, K2, P1, * rep from * to * once, (K1, yo, K2tog) 5 times, K1, P1, K4.
2nd row P2, (P2, K1, P16, K1) 3 times, P4.
3rd row K4, P1, K2, *(K1, yo, K2tog) 4 times, K2, P1, K2, P1, K2,* rep from * to * once, (K1, yo, K2tog) 4 times, K2, P1, K4.
4th row As 2nd row.
5th row K4, P1, K16, P1, K2, P1, (K1, yo, K2tog) 5 times, K1, P1, K2, P1, K16, P1, K4.
6th row P4, K18, P2, K1, P16, K1, P2, K18, P4.
7th row K4, P1, K16, P1, K2, P1, K2, (K1, yo, K2tog) 4 times, K2, P1, K2, P1, K16, P1, K4.
8th row As 2nd row.
Work without shaping until sleeve measures 8½", ending with a RS row. Dec one st at each end of next 5 rows.
Bind off.

■ POCKET

Using larger needles, cast on 25 sts and work in mesh st for 4".
Change to smaller needles and work

in K1, P1 rib for 1¼".
Bind off.

■ PLACKETS (Make 2)

With RS facing, using smaller needles,
pick up and K30 sts down button side
of front opening.
Work 6 rows in K1, P1 rib.
Bind off.
Work buttonhole side as for button
side with the addition of 3 buttonholes
on 3rd row as foll:
Rib 4, (K2tog, yo, rib 8) twice, K2tog,
yo, rib 4.

■ COLLAR

Join shoulder seams.
With RS facing, using smaller needles,
beg at 3rd row of placket, pick up and
K113 sts evenly around neck, ending at
3rd row of placket.
Work in K1, P1 rib for 3½", dec one st
(4 sts in from edge) on every 4th row.
Bind off.

■ FINISHING

Do not press.
Place center of bound-off
edge of sleeve at shoulder
seam and join back
to front at underarm.
Join side and sleeve seams.
Sew on pocket.
Sew on buttons.

CRAZY PAVING

Random shapes of color in vibrant red are separated from each other by wide strips of black to resemble paving stones. The high wrap-up shawl collar gives the garment a quiet sophistication.

■ SIZE

To fit 32-34[36-38]" bust
Figures for larger sizes are given in brackets. Where there is only one set of figures, this applies to all sizes.
See diagram for finished measurements.

■ MATERIALS

Use a lightweight cotton yarn double throughout or a medium weight yarn singly.
18[20]oz/500[500]g main color A (red)
11[12oz]/300[325]g contrast B (black)
One pair each of size 3 and 5 knitting needles *or size to obtain correct gauge*

■ GAUGE

24 sts and 32 rows to 4" over pat using larger needles
To save time, take time to check gauge.

Note

Read chart from right to left for RS rows and left to right for WS rows.
Do not carry colors across; use a separate ball of yarn for each color section. When changing colors, pick up new color from under dropped color to prevent holes (see page 114).

■ STITCHES

Seed st (Main color A)
Worked over even number of sts.
1st row *K1, P1, rep from * to end.

2nd row *P1, K1, rep from * to end.
These 2 rows form pat.
Worked over odd number of sts.
1st row *K1, *P1, K1, rep from * to end.
This row forms pat.

Stockinette st (Color B)
1st row (RS) K.
2nd row P.
These 2 rows form pat.

■ BACK

Using smaller needles, cast on 18[23]A, 8B, 24A, 11B, 45A, 5B, 19[24]A. 130[140] sts.
Keeping to colors as set, work in rib as foll:
1st rib row (RS) K1, *P1, K1, rep from * to end.
2nd rib row P1, *K1, P1, rep from * to end.
Rep last 2 rib rows 12 times.
Change to larger needles and work in pat from chart.
Tie a marker at each end of row 90[106].
Cont without shaping to end of row 180[196].
Bind off.

■ FRONT

Work as for back to end of row 100[118].

Neck shaping
Next row Pat 77[85] sts, turn and leave rem sts on a spare needle.
Keeping side edge straight, shape neck by inc at center front edge as indicated on chart until there are 87[92] sts.

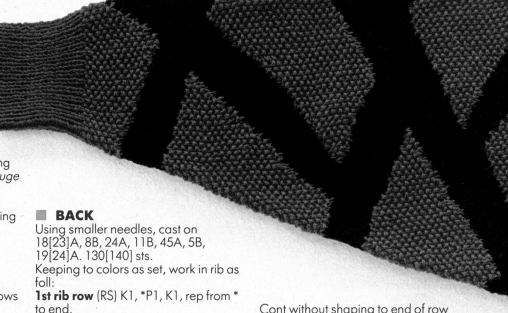

Cont without shaping to end of row 180[196].

Shoulder shaping
Bind off 43[48] sts at beg of next row and cont without shaping on rem 44 sts to end of chart.
With RS facing, rejoin yarns to rem 53[55] sts, cast on 24[30] sts and work to match first side, reversing shapings.

■ SLEEVES

Using smaller needles, cast on 14A, 11B, 33A. 58 sts.
Work in rib as for back for 26 rows.
Change to larger needles and work in pat from chart, shaping sides by inc one st at each end of 3rd and every foll 3rd row until there are 134 sts. Cont without shaping to end of chart.
Bind off.

■ FINISHING

Following manufacturer's directions, block pieces to finished measurements (see page 118).
Join shoulder seams.
Sew bound-off edge of sleeves to front and back between markers.
Join side and sleeve seams.
Join collar at back neck and sew to back neck of body.
Fold collar to wrong side and sew in place.

7[8] 7 7[8]

3½

23½ [24¾]

22 [24¾]

18½

1½

21[23]

FRONT/BACK

22

15½

3

9½

SLEEVE

All measurements are in inches

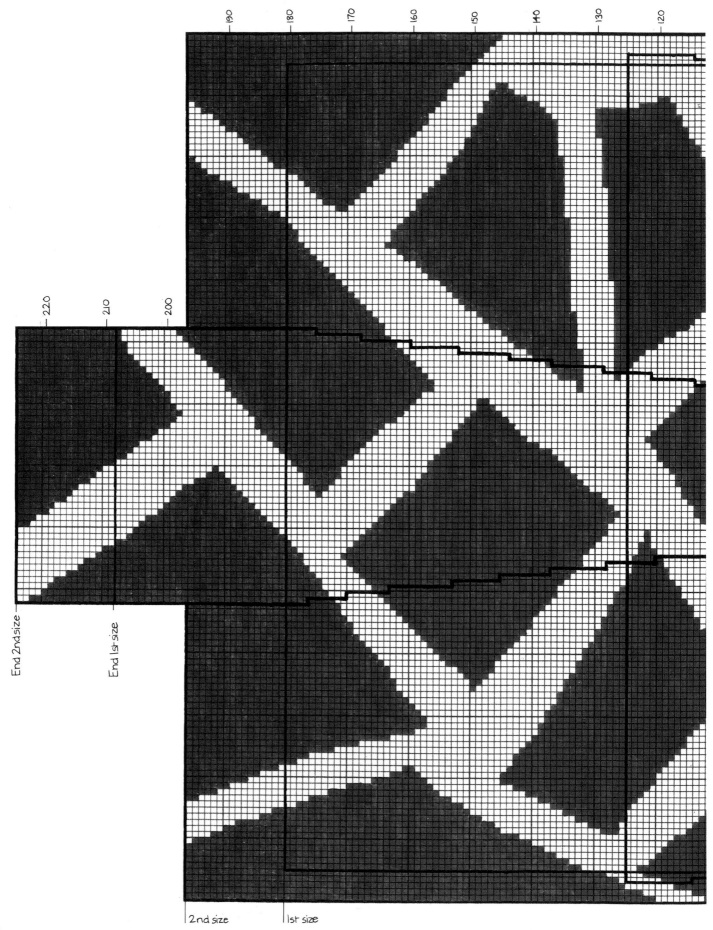

BLOCKBUSTER

Blocks of primary colors provide the background for this striped short-sleeved sweater. Because the yarn in the stripe is woven across the back of the work, it knits up into a closely worked fabric. Long sleeves turn it into a warm winter garment.

■ **SIZE**
To fit 32[34:36:38-40]" bust
Figures for larger sizes are given in brackets. Where there is only one set of figures, this applies to all sizes.
See diagram for finished measurements.

■ **MATERIALS**
Use a lightweight cotton slub yarn.
13[14:14:15]oz/350[375:375:400]g main color A (blue)
3[3:4:4]oz/75[75:100:100]g first contrast B (red)
3[3:4:4]oz/75[75:100:100]g 2nd contrast C (yellow)
6[6:7:7]oz/150[150:175:175]g 3rd contrast D (white)

Long sleeve version:
16[17:17:18]oz/450[475:475:500]g
main color A
One pair each of size 3 and 5 knitting
needles *or size to obtain correct gauge*

■ GAUGE
23 sts and 28 rows to 4" over stripe pat
using larger needles
**To save time, take time to check
gauge.**

Note
Carry D across back of work, weaving
with other color every 2 or 3 sts (see
page 114).

■ BACK
Using smaller needles and A, cast on
113[119:125:131] sts and work in rib
as foll:
1st rib row (RS) K1, *P1, K1, rep from *
to end.
2nd rib row P1, *K1, P1, rep from * to
end.
Rep last 2 rows 3 times, inc one st in
last row. 114[120:126:132] sts.
Change to larger needles and work in
pat as foll:
1st row K5[2:5:2]B, (K1D, K5B)
8[9:9:10] times, K1D, K3B, K3A, K1D,
(K5A, K1D) 8[9:9:10] times,
K5[2:5:2]A.
2nd row P5[2:5:2]A, (P1D, P5A)
8[9:9:10] times, P1D, P3A, P3B, P1D,
(P5B, P1D) 8[9:9:10] times, P5[2:5:2]B.
These 2 rows form pat.
Cont without shaping until end of row
50[51:52:53].
Change color B for C and cont without
shaping until end of row 76, tie a
marker at each end of this row for
armhole.
Cont without shaping until end of row
100[102:104:106].
Change color C for A and cont without
shaping until work measures
8½[9:9½:10]" from armhole marker,
ending with a WS row.

Shoulder shaping
Bind off 6[6:6:0] sts at beg of next
12[8:4:0] rows. 42[72:102:132] sts.
Bind off 0[7:7:7] sts at beg of next
0[4:8:12] rows.
Bind off rem 42[44:46:48] sts.

■ FRONT
Work as for back until front measures
12[14:16:18] rows less than back to
shoulder shaping.

Neck shaping
Next row Pat 46[48:51:53] sts, turn
and leave rem sts on a spare needle.
Bind off 3 sts at beg of next row.
Knit one row.
Bind off 2 sts at beg of next and foll
alternate rows.
Knit one row.
Dec one st at beg of next and foll
2[2:3:3] alternate rows.
Work 0[2:0:2] rows without shaping.
36[38:40:42] sts.

Shoulder shaping
Bind off 6[6:6:0] sts at beg of next and
foll 5[3:1:0] alternate rows.
Work one row.
Bind off 0[7:7:7] sts at beg of next and
foll 0[1:3:5] alternate rows.
With RS facing rejoin yarn to rem sts,
bind off center 22[24:24:26] sts, pat to
end.
Work to match first side reversing
shaping.

■ SLEEVES
**Using smaller needles and A, cast on
77[81:83:85] sts and work in rib as for
back for 8 rows.
Change to larger needles and pat as
foll:
1st row K2[1:2:3]A, (K1D, K5A)
12[13:13:13] times. K1D, K2[1:2:3]A.
This row places stripes**.
Cont in pat, **and at the same time**
shape sides by inc one st at each end
of 5th[5th:5th:4th] and every foll

5th[5th:4th:4th] row 13[13:14:16]
times in all, working inc sts into pat.
103[107:111:117] sts.
Work without shaping until sleeve
measures 11[11½:12:12¼]" from beg,
ending with a WS row.
Bind off.

■ COLLAR
Using smaller needles and with RS
facing and A, beg at center front and
pick up and K99[103:107:111] sts
evenly around neck using a 3rd needle
for ease of working.
Work in rib as for back for 21 rows.
Bind off.

■ FINISHING
Join center front of collar for ⅜" from
neck edge. Press lightly under a cloth.
Join shoulder seams.
Sew sleeves between markers.
Join sleeve and side seams.

LONG SLEEVE VERSION
■ FRONT AND BACK
Work as for short sleeve version.

■ SLEEVES
Work as for short sleeve version from
** to **.
Cont in pat, **and at the same time**
shape sides by inc one st at each end
of every 9th[9th:8th:7th and 8th
alternately]row 13[13:14:16] times in
all, taking inc sts into pat.
103[107:111:117] sts.
Work without shaping until sleeve
measures 17¾", ending with a WS
row.
Bind off.

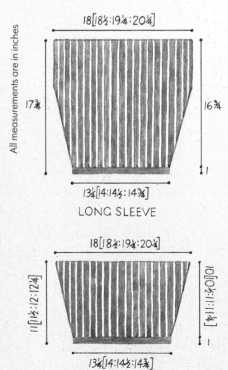

18[18½:19¼:20¼]

17¾   16¾

All measurements are in inches

13¼[14:14½:14¾]
LONG SLEEVE

18[18½:19¼:20¼]

11[11½:12:12¼]   10[10½:11:11¼]

13¼[14:14½:14¾]
SHORT SLEEVE

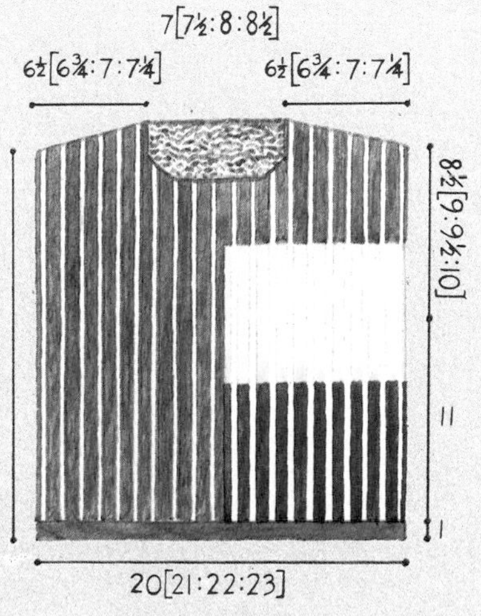

7[7½:8:8½]
6½[6¾:7:7¼]   6½[6¾:7:7¼]

20½[21:21½:22]   8½[9:9½:10]

11

FRONT/BACK

20[21:22:23]

93

BASKETWEAVE

The pattern on this sweater is achieved by the simple technique of slipping stitches. This is one of the easiest ways to create a textured stripe.

■ SIZE
To fit 34[36:38]" bust
Figures for larger sizes are given in brackets. Where there is only one set of figures, this applies to all sizes.
See diagram for finished measurements.

■ MATERIALS
Use a lightweight cotton yarn and a cotton bouclé.
15[15:16]oz/400[400:450]g bouclé A (natural)
9oz/250g first contrast B (slate)
2oz/50g 2nd contrast C (blue)
2oz/50g 3rd contrast D (light blue)
One each of size 3 and 5 circular knitting needle *or size to obtain correct gauge*

■ GAUGE
22 sts and 40 rows to 4" over pat using larger needle
To save time, take time to check gauge.

Note
Body of garment is worked in one piece to armhole.

■ BODY
Using smaller needle and B, cast on 220[236:252] sts and work in rounds of K2, P2 for 2¾".
Change to larger needle and D, knit one round, inc 4 sts evenly.
224[240:256] sts.
Using D, purl one round.
Beg pat as foll:
1st round Using A, K.
2nd round Using A, P.
3rd round Using C, K2, *with yarn at back of work sl 2 p-wise, K6, rep from * to last 6 sts, sl 2 p-wise, K4.
4th to 6th rounds As 3rd round.
7th and 8th rounds As first and 2nd rounds.
9th round As first round.
10th to 12th rounds As 2nd round.
Rep these 12 rounds without shaping until work measures 15½" from beg, using colors C, D and B for 3rd to 6th rounds in rotation.

Back
Divide for armholes as foll:
Keeping pat correct as set, work back and forth across first 112[120:128] sts for back, changing WS rows to K or P as appropriate and leaving rem sts on a spare needle.
Cont on these sts until armhole measures 10", ending with a WS row in A

Front
Rejoin yarn to rem sts on spare needle and work as for back until armhole measures 6¼".

Neck shaping
Next row Pat 41[45:49] sts, turn and leave rem sts on a spare needle.
Dec one st at neck edge on every row until 21[25:29] sts rem.
Work without shaping until front measures same as back.

Leave these 21[25:29] sts on a spare needle.
With RS facing, rejoin yarn to rem sts, bind off center 30 sts and pat to end.
Work to match first side, reversing shaping.
Join shoulders as foll:
Place 21[25:29] sts of front shoulder parallel with 21[25:29] sts of

corresponding back shoulder with WS together and using an extra needle and A, K through back and front and bind off, thus forming a ridge on RS.

■ NECKBAND
With RS facing and using smaller circular needle and B, K70 sts from back neck, pick up and K20 sts down left side of neck, K30 sts across front and K20 sts up right side of neck. 140 sts.
Work in K2, P2 rib for 12 rounds.
Bind off in rib.

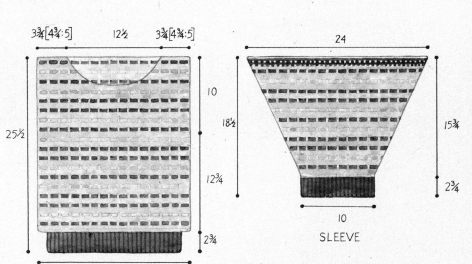

3¾[4¾:5]   12½   3¾[4¾:5]

10

18½

12¾

2¾

25½

20[21¼:23]

FRONT/BACK

24

15¾

2¾

10

SLEEVE

All measurements are in inches

SLEEVES

With RS facing and using larger circular needle and D, beg at start of armhole and pick up and K134 sts evenly around armhole and work back and forth as foll:

1st row Using D, K.

2nd and 3rd rows Using C, K.

4th row Using D, K2, * with yarn at back of work sl 2 p-wise, K2, rep from * to end.

5th row Using D, P2, * with yarn at front of work sl 2 p-wise, P2, rep from * to end.

6th and 7th rows As 4th and 5th rows.

8th and 9th rows Using B, K.

Using B in place of D, rep rows 2-7. Now change to pat as for body using 3rd color for stripe *and keeping pat correct*, dec one st at each end of next and every foll 4th row until sleeve measures approx 15½", ending with an 8th pat row.

Change to smaller needle and D, knit one row dec evenly to 54 sts.

Using D, knit one row.

Change to B, knit one row.

Work in rib as foll:

1st row (WS) P2, *K2, P2, rep from * to end.

2nd row K2, *P2, K2, rep from * to end. Rep these 2 rows until work measures 2¾", ending with a first row. Bind off.

FINISHING

Following manufacturer's directions, block work to finished measurements (see page 118).

Join sleeve seams, matching pat.

95

PRIMARY CABLES

Cables in primary colors provide these vertical stripes. A tailless version is given too.

SIZE

One size to fit up to 38" bust
See diagram for finished measurements.

MATERIALS

Use a lightweight cotton yarn.
23oz/650g main color A (white)
4oz/100g first contrast B (yellow)
2oz/50g 2nd contrast C (red)
2oz/50g 3rd contrast D (blue)
One pair each of size 2 and 4 knitting needles *or size to obtain correct gauge*
One cable needle
Seam binding
Bobbins

GAUGE

24 sts and 32 rows to 4" over pat using larger needles
To save time, take time to check gauge.

Note

Do not carry colors across; use a separate bobbin for each color section. When changing colors, pick up new color from under dropped color to prevent holes (see page 114).

FRONT

Using larger needles and A, cast on 148 sts and work in Rev St st and cable pat as foll:
1st row P19A, K6B, P20A, K6C, P20A, K6B, P20A, K6D, P20A, K6C, P19A.
2nd row and every alternate row K19A, (P6 in contrasting color, K20A) 4 times, P6 in contrasting color, K19A.

3rd and 4th rows As first and 2nd rows.
5th row P19A, slip next 3 sts onto cable needle and leave at back of work, K3B, K3B from cable needle – called C6 –, P20A, C6C, P20A, C6B, P20A, C6D, P20A, C6C, P19A.
  6th row As 2nd row.
    These 6 rows form pat.

Cont in pat without shaping until work measures 12½".
Place a marker at each end of last row.
Cont in pat without shaping until work measures 19½", ending with a WS row.

Neck shaping
Next row Pat 60 sts, turn and leave rem sts on a spare needle.
Bind off 6 sts at neck end of next row.
Work one row.
Bind off 3 sts at neck end of next row.
Work one row.
Bind off 2 sts at neck end of next row.
Work one row.
Dec one st at neck edge on next and 3 foll alternate rows. 45 sts.

Shoulder shaping
Bind off 7 sts at beg of next and 2 foll alternate rows.
Work one row.
Bind off 6 sts at beg of next and 3 foll alternate rows.

All measurements are in inches

With RS facing, rejoin yarn to rem sts, bind off center 28 sts and work to match first side, reversing shaping.

BACK

Using larger needles and A, cast on 22 sts.
1st row Cast on 3 sts, P8A, K6B, P8A. This row sets center cable. Placing further cables as front when sufficient sts have been inc, cont in pat and cast on 3 sts at beg of next 21 rows. 88 sts. Cast on 2 sts at beg of next 30 rows. 148 sts.

Place a marker at each end of last row. Cont without shaping until back measures (from markers) the same as front to shoulder shaping.

Shoulder shaping
Bind off 7 sts at beg of next 6 rows. 106 sts.
Bind off 6 sts at beg of next 8 rows. 58 sts.
Bind off.

SLEEVES

Using smaller needles and A, cast on 83 sts and work in rib as foll:
1st rib row (RS) K1, *P1, K1, rep from * to end.
2nd rib row P1, *K1, P1, rep from * to end.
Rep 2 rib rows 3 times.
Change to larger needles and cable pat as foll:
1st row P1A, K6B, P19A, K6D, P19A, K6B, P19A, K6C, P1A.
This row places cables.
Keeping pat correct and working inc sts into Rev St st only, shape sides by inc one st at each end of 5th and every foll 6th row until there are 129 sts. Cont without shaping until sleeve measures 19½", ending with a WS row. Bind off.

NECKBAND
Join right shoulder seam.
With RS facing and using smaller needles and A, pick up and K127 sts

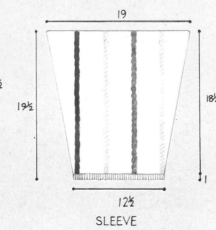

FRONT/BACK

SLEEVE

6¼   8½   6¼
22   9½   12½   6
22½

19
18½
19½
12½
1

evenly around neck edge.
Work 8 rows in rib as for sleeve.
Bind off evenly in rib.

■ BACK RIBBING

With RS facing and using smaller
needles and A, pick up and K173 sts
around tail between markers.
Work 8 rows in rib as for sleeve.
Bind off evenly in rib.

■ FRONT RIBBING

With RS facing and using smaller
needles and A, pick up and K129 sts
across cast on edge.
Work 8 rows in rib as for sleeve.
Bind off evenly in rib.

■ FINISHING

Join left shoulder, using seam binding
tape along the seam (see page 116).
Following manufacturer's directions
block pieces to finished
measurements
(see page 118).
Sew sleeves to back and
front between markers. Join
side and sleeve seams.

TAILLESS VERSION

■ BACK

Work as for front, omitting neck
shaping until back measures same as
front to shoulder shaping.
Shape shoulders as for tail version.

COVER STORY

This versatile design can be worn either as a cardigan or as a beach cover-up. The textured cotton yarn is knitted in to give a terry cloth effect.

■ SIZE
One size to fit up to 40" bust
See diagram for finished measurements.

■ MATERIALS
Use a medium weight cotton yarn and fine terry yarn.
18oz/500g main color A (beige)
11oz/300g first contrast B (yellow)
9oz/250g terry yarn C (beige)
For longer version:
20oz/550g main color A
13oz/350g first contrast B
11oz/300g terry yarn C
One pair each of size 6 and 9 knitting needles *or size to obtain correct gauge*

■ GAUGE
19 sts and 30 rows to 4" over pat using larger needles
To save time, take time to check gauge.

■ BACK
Using smaller needles and A, cast on 109 sts and work in rib as foll:
1st rib row K1A, *P1B, K1A, rep from * to end.
2nd rib row P1A, *K1B, P1A, rep from * to end.
Rep last 2 rows until rib measures 3", ending with a 2nd row.
Change to larger needles and work in pat as foll:
1st row K, using A.
2nd row K, using A.
3rd row K, using C.
4th row P, using C.
5th row P, using B.
6th row K, using B.
7th row K, using C.
8th row P, using C.
These 8 rows form pat.
Cont in pat without shaping until back measures 18½", ending with a WS row.

Armhole shaping
Bind off 8 sts at beg of next 2 rows. 93 sts.
Cont in pat without shaping until armhole measures 7½", ending with a WS row.

Neck shaping
Next row Pat 34 sts, turn and leave rem sts on a spare needle.
Dec one st at neck edge on next and 4 foll alternate rows. 29 sts.
Bind off using A.
With RS facing, rejoin yarn to rem sts, bind off center 25 sts and work to match first side, reversing shaping.

■ LEFT FRONT
Using smaller needles and A, cast on 45 sts and work in rib as for back.
Change to larger needles and work in stripe pat until front measures 17", ending with a RS row.

Front edge shaping
Dec one st at beg of next row and at front edge on every 9th row 7 times, **and at the same time** bind off 8 sts at armhole edge when front measures same as back to armhole. 29 sts.
Cont without shaping until front measures same as back to shoulder.
Bind off using A only.

■ RIGHT FRONT
Work as for left front, reversing shapings.

■ SLEEVES
Using smaller needles and A, cast on 45 sts and work in rib as for back.
Change to larger needles and work in stripe pat, shaping sides by inc one st at each end of every 3rd row 28 times. 101 sts.
Cont without shaping until sleeve measures 18½".

Top shaping
Dec one st at each end of every alternate row 4 times. 93 sts.
Bind off using A only.

■ NECK BORDER
(Worked in 2 halves)
Join shoulder seams.
With RS facing and using smaller needles and A, pick up and K109 sts up right front and across half of back neck.
Work in rib as for back for 4", beg with a 2nd row.
Bind off in rib using A only.
Work 2nd half of border beg at back neck.

■ BELT
Using larger needles and A, cast on 18 sts and work in rib as for back for 67".
Bind off in rib using A only.

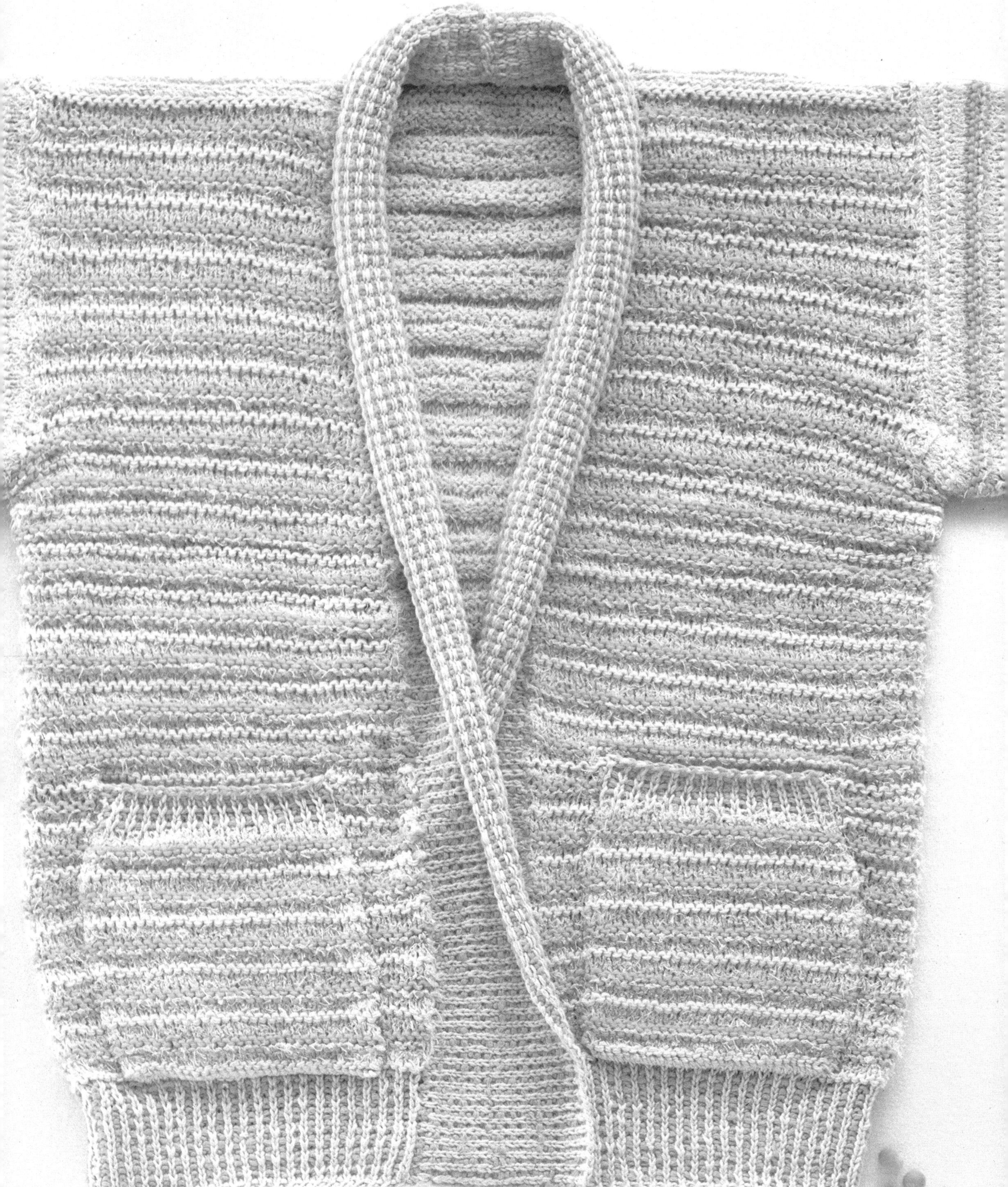

BELT LOOPS (Make 2)
Using larger needles and A, cast on 5 sts and work in rib as for back for 3½". Bind off in rib using A only.

POCKETS (Make 2)
Using larger needles and A, cast on 36 sts and work in stripe pat for 5½". Change to smaller needles and work in rib as for back for 1¼". Bind off in rib using A only.

FINISHING
Following manufacturer's directions, block pieces to finished measurements (see page 118).
Sew in sleeves, joining bound-off edge of sleeves to row ends and top of sleeve shaping to bound-off sts on body.
Join side and sleeve seams.
Join back neck seam of border.
Sew on belt loops.
Sew on pockets.

LONG VERSION

BACK
Using larger needles and A, cast on 109 sts and work in stripe pat as for back of cardigan version until back measures 28½", ending with a WS row.

Armhole and neck shaping
Work as for cardigan version.

LEFT FRONT
Using larger needles and A, cast on 45 sts and work in stripe pat until front measures 27", ending with a RS row.

Front edge shaping
Work as for cardigan version.

RIGHT FRONT
Work as for left front, reversing shapings.

SLEEVES
Work as for cardigan version.

NECK BORDER
(Worked in 2 halves)
Join shoulder seams.
With RS facing and using smaller needles and A, pick up and K123 sts up right front and across half of back neck.
Work in rib as for back for 4", beg with a 2nd row.
Bind off in rib using A only.
Work 2nd half beg at back neck.

BELT, BELT LOOPS AND POCKETS
As cardigan version.

FINISHING
As cardigan version.

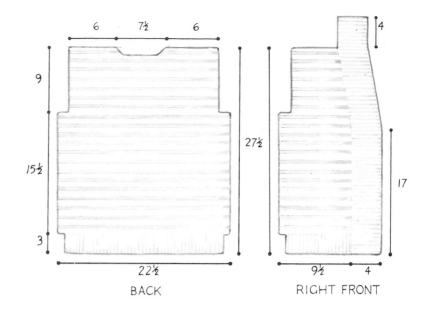

BACK

RIGHT FRONT

All measurements are in inches

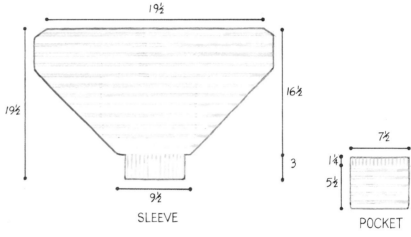

SLEEVE

POCKET

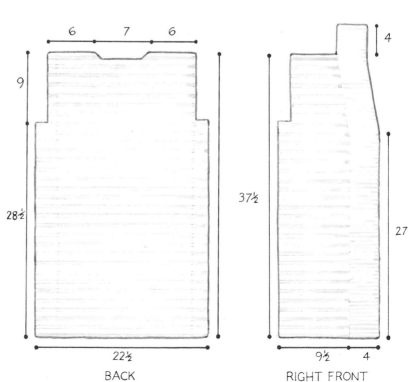

BACK

RIGHT FRONT

SUNSHINE

This textured design is made up of repeating patterns: leaves, an apple tree, an aqueduct and a cable stitch. The crispness of the cotton yarn give the intricate pattern a striking clarity.

■ SIZE
To fit 32-34[36-38:40-42]" bust
Figures for larger sizes are given in brackets. Where there is only one set of figures, this applies to all sizes. *See diagram for finished measurements.*

■ MATERIALS
18[20:22]oz/500[550:600]g fine mercerized cotton yarn
One pair each of size 2 and 4 knitting needles *or size to obtain correct gauge*
One cable needle

■ GAUGE
28 sts and 32 rows to 4" over St st using larger needles
To save time, take time to check gauge.

■ BACK AND FRONT (alike)
Using smaller needles, cast on 114[118:122] sts and work in rib as foll:
1st rib row (RS) K2, *P2, K2, rep from * to end.
2nd rib row P2, *K2, P2, rep from * to end.
Rep last 2 rib rows 16 times.
Inc row K5, * M1, K2, rep from * to last 5 sts, M1, K5. 167[173:179] sts.
Change to larger needles and work in leaf pat as foll:
1st row (WS) K3, *K5, purl into back of st – called P1 tbl –, rep from * to last 2 sts, K2.
2nd row P2, *knit into back of st – called K1 tbl –, P5, rep from * to last 3 sts, P3.
3rd row As first row.
4th row As 2nd row.
5th row As first row.
6th row P2, *(K1, yo, K1) into next st, P5, rep from * to last 3 sts, P3.
7th row K3, *K5, P3, rep from * to last 2 sts, K2.
8th row P1, *(P1, K1) into next st, K1, yo, K1, yo, K1, P2tog, P2, rep from * to last 4 sts, P4.
9th row K2, *K5, P5, rep from * to last 3 sts, K3.
10th row *P2, (P1, K1) into next st, K2, yo, K1, yo, K2, P2tog, rep from * to last 5 sts, P5.
11th row K1, *K5, P7, rep from * to last 4 sts, K4.
12th row P3, *(P1, K1) into next st, K3, yo, K1, yo, K3, P2tog, P2, rep from * to last 2 sts, P2.
13th row K5, *P9, K5, rep from * to end.
14th row P4, *(P1, K1) into next st, slip next 2 sts one at a time k-wise, then insert point of LH needle into fronts of these 2 sts and knit them tog – called ssk –, K5, K2tog, P2tog, P2, rep from * to last st, P1.
15th row K4, * P7, K5, rep from * to last st, K1.
16th row P3, *P2, (P1, K1) into next st, ssk, K3, K2tog, P2tog, rep from * to last 2sts, P2.
17th row K3, *P5, K5, rep from * to last 2 sts, K2.
18th row P4, *P2, (P1, K1) into next st, ssk, K1, K2tog, P2tog, rep from * to last st, P1.
19th row K2, *P3, K5, rep from * to last 3 sts, K3.
20th row P4, *P4, sl 1, K2tog, psso, P1, rep from * to last st, P1.
21st row K.
22nd row P.
23rd row K.
24th row P, inc 3[1:1] sts evenly. 170[174:180] sts.
Now work apple tree pat as foll:
1st row (WS) K0[2:5], (K14, P6, K14) 5 times, K0[2:5].
2nd row K0[2:5], (P14, K6, P14) 5 times, K0[2:5].
Rep last 2 rows 5 times.
13th row As first row.
14th row K0[2:5], (P14, M1, K6, M1, P14) 5 times, K0[2:5].
15th row K0[2:5], (K14, P8, K14) 5 times, K0[2:5].
16th row K0[2:5], (P14, K1, M1, K6, M1, K1, P14) 5 times, K0[2:5].
17th row K0[2:5], (K14, P10, K14) 5 times, K0[2:5].
18th row K0[2:5], (P12, slip next 2 sts onto cable needle and leave at back of work, K2, then P2 from cable needle – called TB4 –, K6, slip next 2 sts onto cable needle and leave at front of work, P2, then K2 from cable needle – called TF4 –, P12) 5 times, K0[2:5].
19th row K0[2:5], (K12, P2, K2, P6, K2, P2, K12) 5 times, K0[2:5].
20th row K0[2:5], (P10, TB4, P2, M1, K6, M1, P2, TF4, P10) 5 times, K0[2:5].
21st row K0[2:5], (K10, P2, K4, P8, K4, P2, K10) 5 times, K0[2:5].

22nd row K0[2:5], (P8, TB4, P4, K1, M1, K6, M1, K1, P4, TF4, P8) 5 times, K0[2:5].
23rd row K0[2:5], (K8, P2, K6, P10, K6, P2, K8) 5 times, K0[2:5].
24th row K0[2:5], (P6, TB4, P4, TB4, K6, TF4, P4, TF4, P6) 5 times, K0[2:5].
25th row K0[2:5], (K6, P2, K6, P2, K2, P6, K2, P2, K6, P2, K6) 5 times, K0[2:5].
26th row K0[2:5], (P6, K2, P4, TB4, P2, K6, P2, TF4, P4, K2, P6) 5 times, K0[2:5].
27th row K0[2:5], (K6, [P2, K4] twice, P6, [K4, P2] twice, K6) 5 times, K0[2:5].
28th row K0[2:5], (P5, K into 2nd st, P first st, slip both sts from needle – called TB2 –, K1B, P2, TB4, P4, K6, P4, TF4, P2, K1 tbl, P into back of 2nd st, K first st, slip both sts from needle – called TF2 –, P5) 5 times, K0[2:5].
29th row K0[2:5], (K5, P1, K1, P1, K2, P2, K6, P6, K6, P2, K2, P1, K1, P1, K5) 5 times, K0[2:5].
30th row K0[2:5], (P4, TB2, P1, [K1, P1, K1, P1, K1] into next st, turn, K5, turn, P5, turn, K2tog, K1, K2tog, turn, sl 1, K2tog, psso – called make bobble or MB –, P2, K2, P4, TB4, K2, TF4, P4, K2, P2, MB, P1, TF2, P4) 5 times, K0[2:5].
31st row K0[2:5], (K2tog, K2, P1, K5, P2, K4 [P2, K2] twice, P2, K4, P2, K5, P1, K2, K2tog) 5 times, K0[2:5].
32nd row K0[2:5], (P2, TB2, P4, TB2, K1 tbl, P2, TB4, P2, K2, P2, TF4, P2, K1 tbl, TF2, P4, TF2, P2) 5 times, K0[2:5].
33rd row K0[2:5], (K2, P1, K5, P1, K1, P1, K2, P2, K4, P2, K4, P2, K2, P1, K1, P1, K5, P1, K2) 5 times, K0[2:5].
34th row K0[2:5], (P2, MB, P4, TB2, P1, MB, P2, K2, P4, K2, P4, K2, P2, MB, P1, TF2, P4, MB, P2) 5 times, K0[2:5].
35th row K0[2:5], (K2tog, K5, P1, K5, [P2, K4] twice, P2, K5, P1, K5, K2tog) 5 times, K0[2:5].
36th row K0[2:5], (P5, TB2, P4, TB2, K1 tbl, P4, K2, P4, K1 tbl, TF2, P4, TF2, P5) 5 times, K0[2:5].
37th row K0[2:5], ([K5, P1] twice, K1, P1, K4, P2, K4, P1, K1, [P1, K5] twice) 5 times, K0[2:5].
38th row K0[2:5], (P5, MB, P4, TB2, P1, MB, P3, TB2, TF2, P3, MB, P1, TF2, P4, MB, P5) 5 times, K0[2:5].

All measurements are in inches

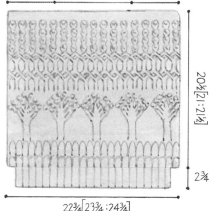

6¼[6¾:7¼]   10¼   6¼[6¾:7¼]

20½[21:21½]

2¾

22¾[23¾:24¾]

FRONT / BACK

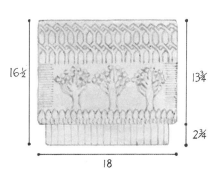

16½

13¾

2¾

18

SLEEVE

39th row K0[2:5], (K2tog, K8, P1, K6, P1, K2, P1, K6, P1, K8, K2tog) 5 times, K0[2:5].
40th row K0[2:5], (P8, TB2, P5, TB2, P2, TF2, P5, TF2, P8) 5 times, K0[2:5].
41st row K0[2:5], (K8, P1, K6, P1, K4, P1, K6, P1, K8) 5 times, K0[2:5].
42nd row K0[2:5], (P8, MB, P5, TB2, P4, TF2, P5, MB, P8) 5 times, K0[2,5].
43rd row K0[2:5], (K2tog, K12, P1, K6, P1, K12, K2tog) 5 times, K0[2:5].
44th row K0[2:5], (P13, MB, P6, MB, P13) 5 times, K0[2:5].
45th row K.
46th row P.
Rep last 2 rows twice.

First size only:
Next row K2tog, K31, (K2tog, K32) 3 times, K2tog, K31, K2tog.
164 sts.

2nd size only:
Next row K86, K2tog, K86. 173 sts.

3rd size only:
Next row (K1, P1) into first st, K to last st, (K1, P1) into last st. 182 sts.

All sizes:
Now work aqueduct pat as foll:
1st row (RS) P2, *P3, (K1 tbl, K1) into next st, then insert LH needle point behind the vertical strand that runs downward from between the 2 sts just made, and K1 tbl into this strand to make 3 sts from one – called inc 2 –, P5, rep from * to end.
2nd row *K5, P3, K3, rep from * to last 2 sts, K2.
3rd row P2, *P3, K1, sl 1, K1, P5, rep from * to end.
Rep last 2 rows 3 times.
10th row As 2nd row.
11th row P2, *P3, K1, inc 2, K1, P5, rep from * to end.
12th row K5, P2, K1, P2, *K8, P2, K1, P2, rep from * to last 5 sts, K5.
13th row P2, *P2, slip one st onto cable needle and leave at back of work, K2, then K1 from cable needle – called BKC –, P1, slip 2 sts onto cable needle and leave at front of work, K1, then K2 from cable needle – called FKC –, P4, rep from * to end.
14th row K4, P2, P1 tbl , K1, P1 tbl, P2, K1, *K5, P2, P1 tbl, K1, P1 tbl, P2, K1, rep from * to last 3 sts, K3.
15th row *P3, slip one st onto cable needle and leave at back of work, K2, then P1 from cable needle – called BPC –, K1 tbl, P1, K1 tbl, slip 2 sts onto cable needle and leave at front of work, P1, then K2 from cable needle – called FPC –, P1, rep from * to last 2 sts, P2.
16th row *K3, P2, [K1, P1 tbl] twice, K1, P2, K1, rep from * to last 2 sts, K2.
17th row P1, * slip 2 sts onto cable needle and leave at back of work, K2, then K2 from cable needle – called BC4 –, (P1, K1 tbl) twice, P1, slip 2 sts onto cable needle and leave at front of work, K2, then K2 from cable needle – called FC4 –, rep from * to last st, P1.

18th row K1, *P2, (K1, PB1) 4 times, K1, P2, rep from * to last st, K1.
19th row P1, K2, *(P1, K1 tbl) 4 times, P1, FC4, rep from * to last 12 sts, (P1, K1 tbl) 4 times, P1, K2, P1.
20th row K1, *P2, (K1, P1 tbl) 4 times, K1, P2, rep from * to last st, K1.
21st row P1, *TF4, (P1, K1 tbl) twice,

P1, TB4, rep from * to last st, P1.
22nd row K2, *K1, P2, (K1, P1 tbl) twice, K1, P2, K3, rep from * to end.
23rd row P2, *P1, TF4, P1, TB4, P3, rep from * to end.
24th row *K5, ssk, K3tog, pass ssk over the K3tog – called dec 5 –, K3, rep from * to last 2 sts, K2.
These 24 rows form aqueduct pat.
Rep pat once more.
Work 4 rows in Rev St st.
Back should now measure approx 19".
Next row P2tog, P to last 2 sts, P2tog. 162[171:180] sts.
Now work in cable pat as foll:
1st row (WS) *K2, P1, K3, P1, K2, rep from * to end.
2nd row *P2, K1, P3, K1, P2, rep from * to end.
3rd row As first row.
4th row *P2, K1, P1, MB, P1, K1, P2, rep from * to end.
5th row As first row.
6th row As 2nd row.
7th row As first row.
8th row *P2, yarn to back of work between 2 needles – called yb –, sl 1, yarn to front of work between 2 needles – called yfwd –, P3, yb, sl 1, yfwd, P2, rep from * to end.
9th row K2, yfwd, sl 1, yb, K3, yfwd, sl 1, yb, K2, rep from * to end.
10th row P2, slip 4 sts onto cable needle and leave at back of work, K1, then K4 from cable needle – called T5 –, P2, rep from * to end.
11th row *K2, P1, K3, P1, K2, rep from * to end.

12th row *P2, K1, P3, K1, P2, rep from * to end.
These 12 rows form cable pat.
Rep these 12 rows until back measures 22½[23:23½]", ending with a WS row.
Work 6 rows in seed st.
Bind off very loosely.

SLEEVES
Using smaller needles, cast on 62 sts and work 28 rows in rib as for back, ending with a 2nd row.
Inc row (K1, P1, K1) into first st, *M1, K1, rep from * to end. 125 sts.
Change to larger needles and work rows 1-21 of leaf pat.
Next row (K1, P1) into first st, P to end. 126 sts.
Work rows 1-44 of apple pat, but knit 12 extra sts at each side instead of 0[2:5].
Next row (P1, K1) into first st, K to last st, (K1, P1) into last st. 128 sts.
Work rows 1-24 of aqueduct pat twice.
Sleeve should measure approx 16½".
Bind off very loosely.

FINISHING
Join shoulder seams, leaving 10¼" open for neck.
Tie marker 9" down from shoulder seam on back and front, and sew bound-off edge of sleeve between markers.
Join side and sleeve seams.

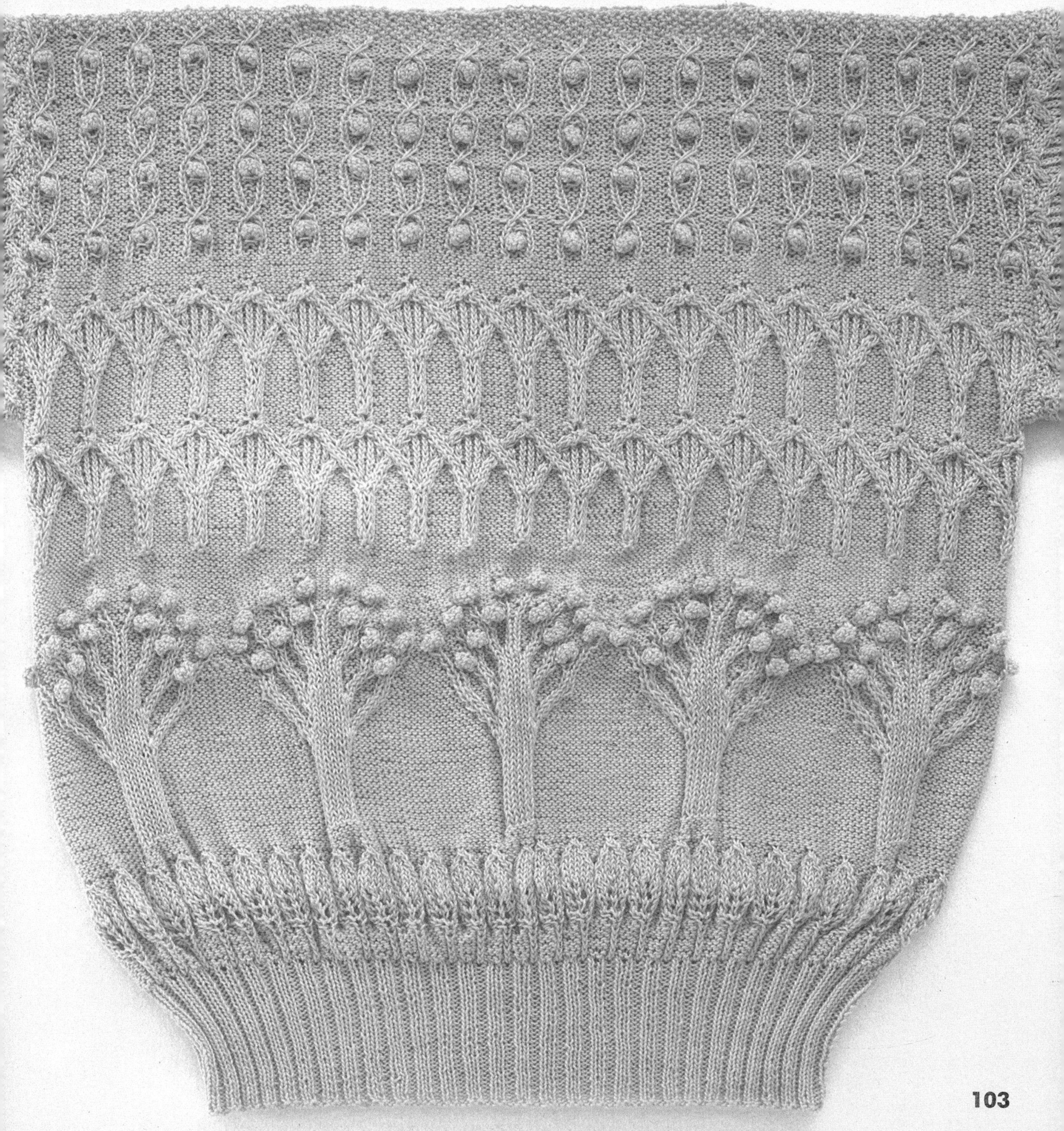

HOT SHOT

Easy to knit and fun to wear, this simple short top is knitted in cotton tape. The depth of the V at the back can be adjusted by simply altering the position of the buttons.

■ SIZE

One size to fit up to 38" bust
See diagram for finished measurements.

■ MATERIALS

11oz/300g cotton tape 10mm wide
One pair each of size 11 and 15 knitting needles *or size to obtain correct gauge*
One size F crochet hook
Two 1½" buttons

■ GAUGE

11 sts and 15 rows to 4" over g st using larger needles
To save time, take time to check gauge.

■ FRONT

Using smaller needles, cast on 46 sts and work 2 rows in g st.
Change to larger needles and continue in g st, inc one st at each end of 12th and every foll 14th row 5 times in all. 56 sts.
Bind off.

■ LEFT BACK

Using smaller needles, cast on 30 sts and work 2 rows in g st.
Change to larger needles and cont in g st, shaping sides by dec one st at end of 2nd and every 4th row, **and at the same time** inc one st at beg of 12th and every 14th row until back measures same as front. 18 sts.
Bind off.

■ RIGHT BACK

Work as for left back, reversing shapings and working buttonholes on 6th row from cast-on edge as foll:
1st buttonhole row K3, bind off next 2 sts, K5, bind off next 2 sts, K to end.
2nd buttonhole row K, casting on 2 sts over those bound off on previous row.

■ FINISHING

Join shoulder seams.
Join side seams leaving 7" for armhole.
Using crochet hook, work one row of single crochet around armholes, up right back, around front neck and down left back to prevent stretching.
Sew on buttons.

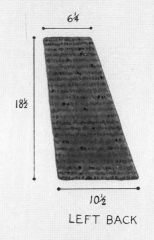

6¼

18½

10½

LEFT BACK

20

18½

16½

FRONT

All measurements are in inches

SNAKES & LADDERS

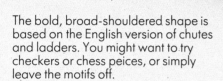

The bold, broad-shouldered shape is based on the English version of chutes and ladders. You might want to try checkers or chess peices, or simply leave the motifs off.

■ SIZE
One size to fit up to 40" bust
See diagram for finished measurements.

■ MATERIALS
Use a lightweight cotton yarn and cotton slub.
16oz/450g slub yarn main color A (white)
16oz/450g slub yarn main color B (black)
1oz/25g contrasting cotton yarn C (pink)
One pair of size 3 knitting needles
One 30"-long circular size 8 knitting needle *or size to obtain correct gauge*
Two shoulder pads

■ GAUGE
17 sts and 25 rows to 4" over St st using larger needles
To save time, take time to check gauge.

Note
Read chart from right to left for RS knit rows and left to right for WS purl rows. Unless stated St st is used throughout. Do not carry colors across; use a separate bobbin of yarn for each color section. When changing colors, pick up new color from under dropped color to prevent holes (see page 114). The rib of the body is included in the chart.

■ FRONT
Using smaller needles, cast on 100 sts using A and B alternately as on chart. Work from row 1 of chart in K1, P1 rib for 1¼".
Change to circular needle and cont without shaping to end of row 80.

Sleeve shaping
Inc one st at each end of next and foll 5th row. 104 sts.
Work 4 rows without shaping.

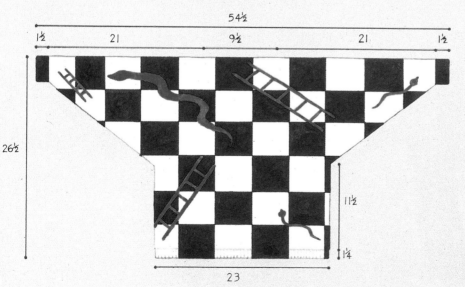

54½
1½   21   9½   21   1½

26½

11½

1¼

23

FRONT/BACK

All measurements are in inches

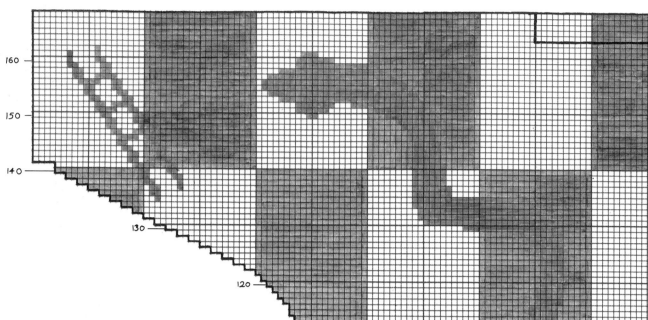

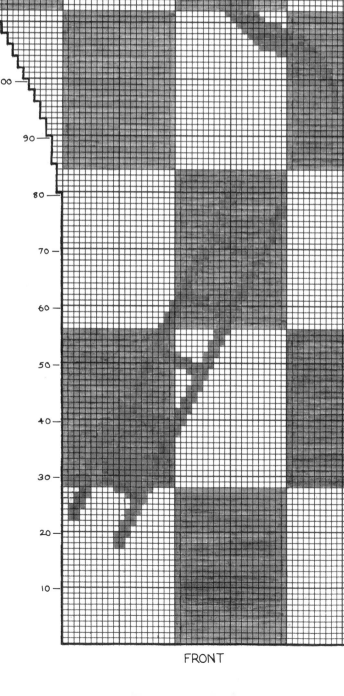

Inc one st at each end of next and foll
3rd row. 108 sts.
Work 2 rows without shaping.
Inc one st at each end of next and foll 9
alternate rows. 128 sts.
Inc one st at each end of next 6 rows.
140 sts.
Inc 2 sts (by working 3 times into st) at
each end of next 18 rows. 212 sts.
Cast on 4 sts at beg of next 2 rows. 220
sts.
Cont without shaping until end of row
164.
Next row Work 90 sts in St st, work
center 40 sts in K1, P1, rib, work in St st
to end.
Rep last row twice.
Next row Pat 90 sts, bind off center 40
sts in rib, pat to end.
Leave rem sts on a spare needle.

■ BACK
Work as for front, working mirror
image by reversing order of colors and
working checks only (omitting chutes
and ladders).
Join shoulders as foll:
Place front and back together with
right sides facing and using an extra
needle, K through back and front and
bind off.
Bind off rem shoulder as first.

■ CUFFS
With RS facing and using smaller
needles pick up and K40 sts evenly
along sleeve edge using B for front of
wrist and A for back wrist.
Work 1½" in K1, P1 rib.
Bind off loosely in rib.

■ FINISHING
Join underarm and side seams.
Following manufacturer's directions,
block sweater to finished
measurements (see page 118).
Insert shoulder pads.

FRONT

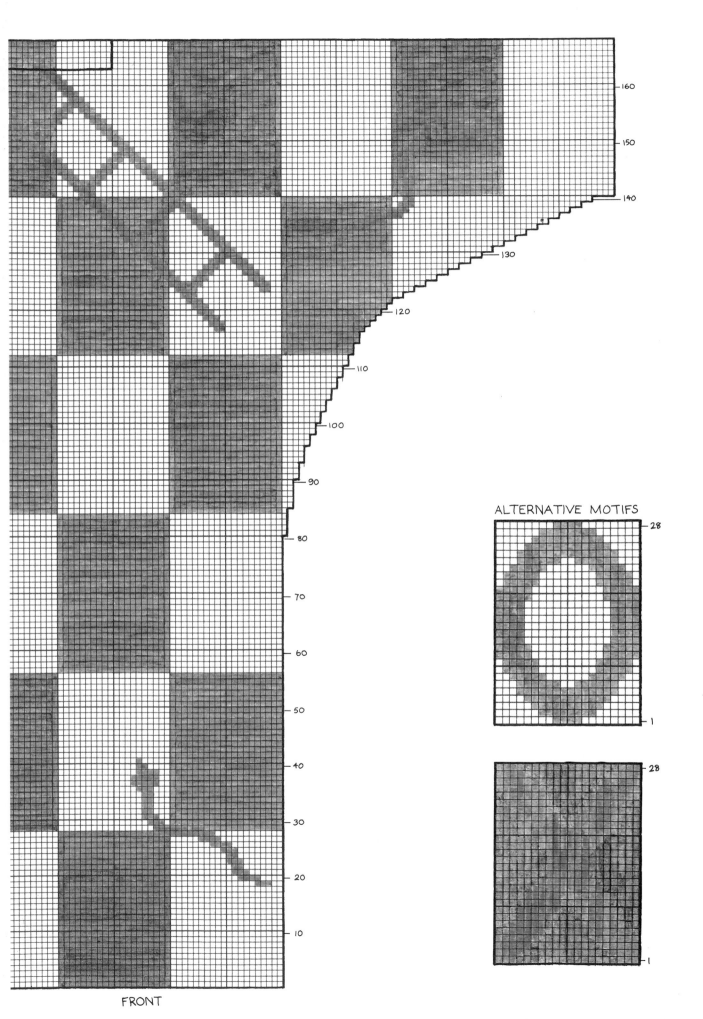

160

150

140

130

120

110

100

90

80

70

60

50

40

30

20

10

ALTERNATIVE MOTIFS

28

1

28

1

FRONT

109

GAUGE & MEASUREMENTS

On the following nine pages, we concentrate on useful hints for good knitting and how to achieve a professional finish with cotton. We are assuming that the reader already has a good knowledge of basic knitting techniques. A right-handed knitter is shown in the illustrations. If you are left-handed, prop the book up in front of a mirror: you can then interpret the method without difficulty. Some of the designers in this book specify certain techniques and finishes in their instructions; others do not. You can choose from those illustrated here.

▥ NEEDLE SIZES

American	15	13	11	–	–	10½	10	9	8	7	6	5	4	3	2	1	0
Metric	10	9	8	7½	7	6½	6	5½	5	4½	4	3¾	3¼	3	2¾	2¼	2
English	000	00	0	1	2	3	4	5	6	7	8	9	10	11	12	13	14

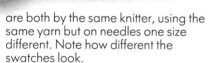

▥ GAUGE

The gauge of your knitting is determined by the type of yarn used, how thick or thin it is, the size of needles and the amount of yarn pulled through for every stitch – that is, the tension –, which varies from knitter to knitter and with beginners is not usually consistent. The two samples of knitting pictured below illustrate the difference a change in needle size makes. They

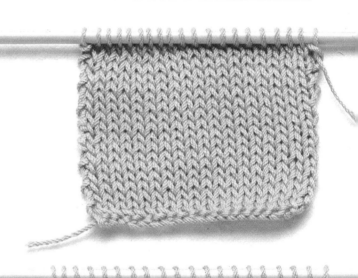

are both by the same knitter, using the same yarn but on needles one size different. Note how different the swatches look.

The stitch gauge of a garment is given at the beginning of every pattern. It specifies the number of stitches and rows over a 4" square on the designer's knitted fabric. If your knitting cannot match this stitch gauge, the fit and shape of your finished garment will not correspond to the illustrated design and measurement diagram. There is a risk that the garment might change drastically in length or width, and your work would be spoiled.

▥ MAKING A GAUGE SWATCH

Before starting to knit any design, you need to make a gauge swatch. Work with the size needles and the yarn type and weight stated in the pattern. Knit the main pattern stitches of the garment for a square measuring about 5" and bind off. It is important to reproduce the main pattern exactly because this will influence the gauge. Any cables or color changes, for example, should be included.

Lay the square out flat (do not block first) and measure the number of rows per 4" and the number of stitches per 4". Having taken this reading, wash, dry and block the square and measure it again to make sure that washing doesn't alter the gauge. (Cotton sometimes "bulks up" when washed and it might not return to the original gauge.)

If your gauge reading is different from that specified in the pattern, the simplest way to rectify this is by using a different size needle. To obtain fewer stitches and rows per 4", use a larger needle, and to obtain more, use a smaller needle until you have the correct gauge for the pattern Even if your gauge is only slightly different, this difference will be increased over the whole garment.

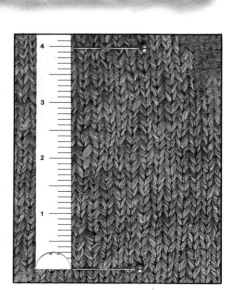

▣ READING CHARTS

Each square of the charts in this book represents a stitch, and each line corresponds to a row of knitting. The color changes are indicated on each square of the chart.

To knit from a chart, read from the right-hand corner to the left for the right side of your design, and from left to right of the chart for the wrong side. To make it easier to keep track of the pattern, place a ruler under each row as you knit it. If you want to substitute a different motif or your own design on a pullover, this is easily done by transferring a charted or squared design (say from a source such as cross stitch embroidery or needle point), which you then draw freehand onto a chart within the outline of your

pullover, or onto graph paper. It is important to understand that although the chart is marked in squares, stitches themselves are not square. They are usually wider than they are long, so a successful design may appear slightly longer on the chart in proportion to the width than it will appear on the finished garment.

If you are working with a chart that doesn't show the outline of the whole garment but represents only a small, repeated section – such as Fair Isle (see page 18) – and you need to increase for shaping, any increases must be incorporated into new repeats of the pattern.

The chart on the left is shown knitted below.

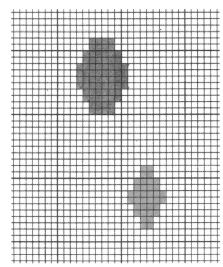

▣ MEASUREMENTS

Knitting designs have varying amounts of ease written into the pattern instructions. A jacket, for example, will have a deeper armhole than a pullover, so that there is plenty of room for other clothes underneath it; a loose T-shirt design will measure far more around the bust than the actual body measurement; tight ribbing will be constructed so that it stretches when worn and shrinks back when taken off.

The measurement diagrams with each pattern in this book include ease and are not measurements that relate directly to body measurements. It is important for you to decide at the outset whether you want the garment to be figure-hugging or loose-fitting.

To insure a baggier sizing, knit a garment that measures at least 4" more than your own bust measurement. In some designs, only one size is given to fit up to a certain bust size. To calculate your size and fashion requirements, you should record the following body measurements:

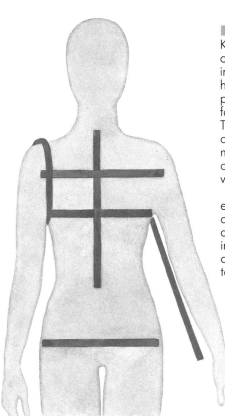

ABBREVIATIONS

approx	approximately
beg	begin(ning)
cont	continu(e)(ing)
dec	decreas(e)(ing)
foll	follow(s)(ing)
g st	garter stitch
g	gram(s)
inc	increas(e)(ing)
K	knit
k-wise	knitwise
LH	left hand (needle)
mm	millimeter(s)
oz	ounce(s)
psso	pass slipped stitch(es) over
pat	pattern
P	purl
p-wise	purlwise
rem	remain(s)(ing)
rep	repeat(ing)
Rev St st	Reverse Stockinette stitch
RH	right hand (needle)
rib	ribbing
RS	right side
sc	single crochet
sl	slip(ped)
st(s)	stitch(es)
St st	Stockinette stitch
tbl	through back of loop(s)
tog	together
WS	wrong side
yb	yarn to back of work
yo	yarn over (needle)
yfwd	yarn forward
M1	make one st by picking up horizontal loop lying before next st and working into the back of it.
*	repeat instructions following or between *
( )	repeat instructions inside parentheses
†	directions that appear between indicate a separate pattern stitch

Any other abbreviations are explained in the text for each design.

1 Bust, around fullest part of bust.
2 Back length, nape of neck to waist or point to which garment extends.
3 Shoulder width, across back at shoulder blades.
4 Underarm, from armpit to where finished garment should end.
5 Hip, at the widest part.
6 Armhole.
Check these measurements, where appropriate, against the measurement diagram and calculate which size you want to knit.

BASIC TECHNIQUES

■ CASTING ON

Casting on forms the first row of loops of the knitted fabric. It is important that the stitches be of an even size to produce a neat edge. Different casting on methods are suitable for particular types of finish. Some garments require

an elastic edge, others a firm edge or even an invisible edge. The relative non-elasticity of cotton requires a firmer edge than other types of yarn.

If you want to add a hem or to work the ribbing onto the sleeve or body of the garment afterward, cast on in the

usual way and knit the body of the garment. When you have finished the knitting, use a knitting needle to pick up and knit the loops from the cast on edge on the right side of the garment. These will become the first row of knitting for the hem or ribbing. This is particularly useful if the ribbing stretches with washing and wearing – you can then unravel it and redo it.

■ SLIP LOOP

1

2

3

The slip loop is the first stitch to cast on. Wind a length of yarn around two fingers and then a second time, taking the yarn to the back of the first loop,

away from you (1). Using either a needle or your other hand, bring the second loop through the first loop (2) and by pulling the two ends of yarn,

tighten the loop on the needle (3). The remaining stitches can be cast on using your usual method – either with two needles or with your thumb.

■ CABLE CAST ON

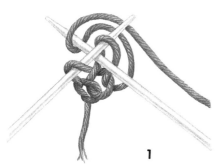

1

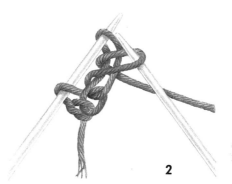

2

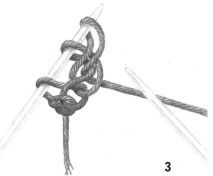

3

This gives an elastic and decorative edge. This method is worked with two needles. Start with a slip loop; cast on one more stitch by knitting into the slip loop and slipping the new stitch back

onto the left-hand needle. Insert the right-hand needle *between* the slip loop and the new cast-on stitch (1). Take the yarn around the needle and pull through a new stitch (2) and slip

the new stitch back onto the left-hand needle (3).

If you want to emphasize the rope-like edge that this creates, use two strands of yarn for the cast-on row.

■ INVISIBLE CAST ON

This cast-on method gives a single ribbed edge that looks very professional, almost like a machine-

knitted edge. It is ideal for cardigans and vests.

You will need a length of contrasting yarn. With the length of contrasting

yarn make a slip loop and cast on half the number of stitches specified in the pattern you have chosen to knit plus one extra stitch. Now change to your chosen yarn and follow this pattern for the first 6 rows (1), then revert to the master pattern for the required length of ribbing.

1st row K1, *yo, K1, rep from * to end.
2nd row K1, *yarn to front of work between needles (yft), sl 1, yarn to back of work between needles (yb), K1, rep from * to end.
3rd row Sl 1, *yb, K1, yft, sl 1, rep from * to end.
4th row As 2nd row.
5th row As 3rd row.
6th row K1, *P1, K1, rep from * to end. Remove contrasting yarn (2).

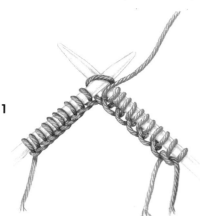

1

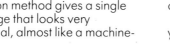

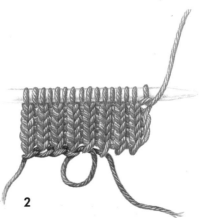

2

EDGES

Gauge is just as important on the edges of your knitting as on the main body of the garment.

To make a firm cast-on edge, knit into the back of the stitches on the first row (except when you cable cast on; in which case knit into the front).

When binding off, use the same stitches as those you have been working over the pattern.

The left and right edges of a garment (known as selvedges) can be decorative where they will show but must be firm where they are enclosed for a neat seam. Decorative selvedges

are worked over two stitches on each side to prevent the fabric from curling. The second and next to last stitch on every knit row are purled.

Selvedges to be seamed or from which stitches will be picked up later are worked over one stitch on each side as shown below.

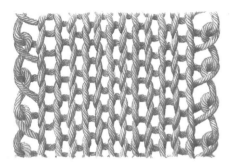

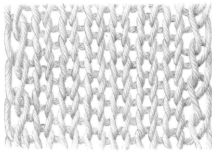

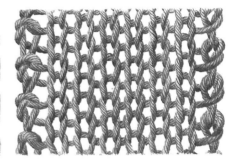

The most common method of working the selvedge is merely to knit all stitches on knit rows and purl them on purl rows.

To make a chain edge, slip the first and last stitch of every knit row knitwise. Purl all stitches on the purl row.

The slip stitch edge forms a neat base for picking up stitches. Slip the first stitch of every row knitwise and knit the last stitch of every row.

CROCHET BIND OFF

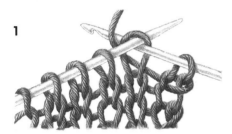

The crochet bind off is a good method to use with cotton, since it is less likely to produce too tight an edge. Using a crochet hook, knit the first stitch. Take

the yarn to the back of the work and insert the crochet hook through the front of the next stitch (1). With the crochet hook, draw the yarn through

the second and first stitches (2). Retain this stitch on the hook (3) and repeat the process until all stitches have been bound off.

INVISIBLE BIND OFF

The invisible bind off method is used when further knitting is to be added later on. Cut the main yarn, leaving a length longer than the width of the main knitting. Thread the yarn through a tapestry needle and draw it through the stitches on the last row of knitting. Secure the yarn by knotting through the last loop. When you come to complete the garment, pick up the stitches, withdraw the threaded yarn and rejoin a new ball of yarn.

CIRCULAR KNITTING

In circular knitting the work progresses in rounds, producing a tubular fabric with only two edges – top and bottom. Tubular fabric can be knitted on three or more double-pointed needles with an extra needle for the knitting itself. One circular needle with rigid points at each end and a flexible length between them is particularly suitable for sleeves or a large piece of work.

A round is complete when all the stitches have been knitted back to the first cast-on stitch. To close the circle, knit into the first cast-on stitch, which will be marked by the free end of yarn. All rounds, color changes and pattern changes begin and end at this point.

When working with several needles, it may be easier to cast all the stitches onto one needle and then divide the stitches equally between the number of needles you are using. Make sure that the same number of stitches is kept on each needle while knitting.

Some of the designs in this book are knitted in one piece to the armholes or the body and sleeves are knitted in one piece. A flexible circular needle is very useful when trying to manage such a large number of stitches and such a weight of fabric. However, if you are knitting a cardigan, for example, you must turn the work and knit back and forth in rows even though you are using a circular needle. Once you become accustomed to using circular needles, you may find them easier for all your knitting.

ELASTIC IN RIBBING

A useful technique for insuring firm fitting ribbing is to knit in shirring elastic across the back of the ribbing. Twist the elastic around the main yarn every two stitches of knitting and on every row, making sure you maintain the correct gauge; don't pull the elastic tight. To elasticize ribbing at the end of knitting see page 118.

113

JOINING IN YARN

Many of the designs in this book have used more than one color of yarn. Joining in a new color and working the yarn, when not in use, into the back of the fabric are techniques that need to be mastered if the garment is to look good and wear well.

You must be careful to choose the method most appropriate to the yarn and the garment. For example, if you make a cotton summer top and weave the yarn not in use across the back of the work, the top may become heavy because of the strands of extra yarn and too warm for your purposes. Similarly, if you strand yarns across too many stitches, the loose strands may catch on jewelry and ruin the garment.

Unless you are creating an isolated area of color, it is never advisable to join yarn in the middle of a row. It has a tendency to distort the stitches where it is joined. Always make sure you have enough yarn to finish a row and then join a new ball or color at the side edge.

Work the first few stitches with the new yarn. Tie the old yarn to the new to secure it until you join the seams and darn in all the loose ends. Similarly, you can knit in the loose ends as you go to save time later.

It should only be necessary to join a new ball of yarn in the middle of a row if you are working on an isolated area of color. Work the first stitch with the new yarn, leaving long enough loose ends to darn in later. Always remember to cross the two colors over to prevent a hole from forming – a technique known as intarsia.

When joining yarn in the middle of a row, it is neater to knit the loose end of the new yarn into the work as you go. This cuts down on the time you need to finish the garment.

■ INTARSIA

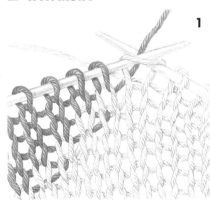

1

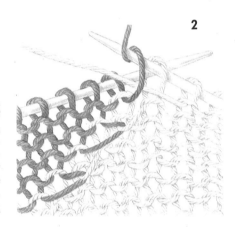

2

This method is also known as crossing colors – every color being worked has its own ball of yarn for each area. This is used when isolated areas of color appear on the fabric or when the same colors occur at some distance from each other. Yarns are crossed over at the join with the neighboring color so that no hole forms. If you are using a large number of colors over small areas, it is easiest to use lengths of yarn or bobbins of yarn instead of balls to avoid tangling.

On a knit row (1), pick up the new yarn from under the old yarn and drop the old yarn to the back of the work. Continue knitting with the new color.

On a purl row (2), cross the new yarn with the old yarn in the same way.

Intarsia fabrics are very neat with few loose ends, and they can often look virtually the same on both sides.

■ COLOR INSERTIONS

One way of inserting blocks of contrast color is with a technique called "short rows" or "turning". The method involves knitting across a certain number of stitches (as specified in the pattern), turning the work and leaving the remaining stitches unworked until the color insertion is completed. At the beginning of every "short" or "turned" row, the first stitch is slipped and the next worked tightly to prevent a hole from forming. When the insertion is completed, pick up and knit across the remaining stitches. Because this type of insertion creates extra rows of knitting, the color shapes are usually staggered across the work to compensate (see page 50).

This strip of inserted color is worked using only one ball of yarn at a time.

■ STRANDING

It is very important to maintain the correct gauge when using this technique. It is easy to pull the floating yarns at the back of the work too tightly, and this causes the fabric to pucker. Check your gauge as you work by flattening out the knitting to see if there are any tight areas.

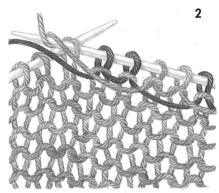

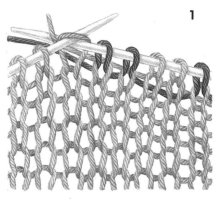

The wrong side shows the neat strands of the two colors in this checked garment.

Stranding does restrict the stretch of a garment. It is not advisable to strand the yarn over more than five stitches in a row, because the loops will catch and distort the garment or break off and create holes in the knitted fabric.

When stranding the yarn on a knit row (1), knit the required number of stitches in the main color and drop the yarn to the back of the work. Knit the next stitches in the contrasting color and drop the contrasting yarn to the

back of the work. Continue in this way, allowing the unused yarn to float across the back of the work. If you pull the first stitch in a new color too tightly, you will pucker the work. When stranding on a purl row (2), bring the yarns to the front of the work and work as for a knit row, but keeping the floating yarns at the front. You will find you can build up speed by using your index finger for one color and another finger for the other color.

■ WEAVING IN

This is the method used for designs with frequent large repeats where five or more stitches separate a color repeat, or where several colors have to be worked in one row. It is important to avoid long floats across the back of the work. These catch, causing holes and distortions. By weaving in, you can produce a well-finished fabric, but the more colors you carry across the back of the work, the thicker and warmer the fabric will be. If there are only a couple of repeats and they are far apart, it might be sensible to cross the colors (intarsia) and use separate balls of yarn for each area. It is also very important to keep to your correct gauge when weaving in. Looser rather than tighter weaving in is advisable. Check that the woven-in yarns are not showing through the work.

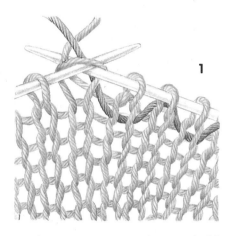

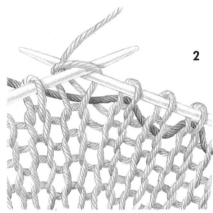

The reverse side of the work should look as though the yarn has been threaded through the back of the work.

When weaving in on a knit row, hold the main yarn as you would normally and the contrasting yarn with the forefinger of your other hand. Knit one stitch with the main yarn, feeding the contrasting yarn over the stitch as you work (1). Knit the next stitch over the

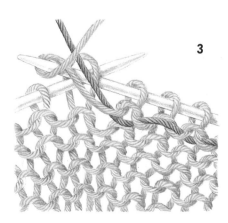

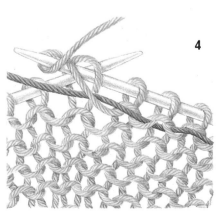

contrasting yarn (2). When weaving in on a purl row, work as for a knit row but keep the yarns at the front of the work. Feed the contrasting yarn over the main yarn and work one stitch (3), then purl the next stitch keeping the contrasting yarn below the main yarn (4).

■ RIBBING DESIGNS

So often the use of multicolored patterns is restricted to the body of the garment and sometimes the sleeves. Some of the designs in this book have the color scheme extended into the ribbing too.

Top left: *A simple method of introducing color into the ribbing of the body of the garment and the sleeves is to cast on in a contrasting yarn. This is particularly effective if the contrast is used again in the design – as for example, on "Tiger Tails" (see page 81).*

Top right: *The "Balloons" sweater (see page 34) has horizontal stripes of the contrasting colors across the ribbing.*

Bottom left: *The two main colors of the design have been worked for the purl and knit stitches in the ribbing on the "Checkerboard" cardigan (see page 61).*

Bottom right: *Some brands are worked in a long narrow strip and sewn onto the body of the garment when the seams are joined. This method has been used on "Zigzag" (see page 22); the colors were worked in rows of knit and purl to imitate the ribbed effect. It is easier to work striped bands in this way.*

FINISHING

However beautifully a garment has been knitted, unless time and care are taken over the finishing stages, the garment will look unattractive and the effort spent on the knitting itself will have been wasted.

■ JOINING SEAMS

Certain seam finishes are especially appropriate to certain weights of yarn and garment. Sometimes the seam can be used as a decorative feature.

Edge to edge seam (1)

This achieves an almost invisible edge and is useful for ribbing and cuffs. As they will be visible, the selvedges to be joined must be neat and have an equal number of rows.

Place the pieces to be joined wrong side up and butt the edges together. Using a tapestry needle to avoid splitting the stitches, thread it with a length of matching yarn. Work from side to side, taking the needle through the edge stitch on both sides. Continue this stitch along the length of the seam.

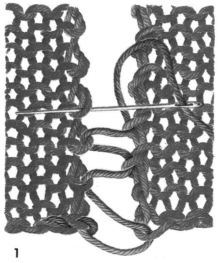
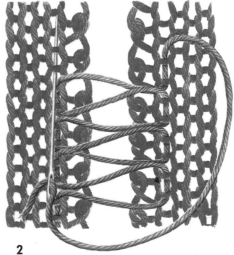

1

2

Mattress stitch (2)

This is a neat seam which is worked from the right side. Placing right sides uppermost, on a flat surface, butt both pieces to be joined edge to edge. Insert the threaded tapestry needle

through the two bar loops next to the selvedge stitch and take the needle across to the other edge. Continue working from side to side for the whole seam. The selvedge itself will be hidden by the overcasting.

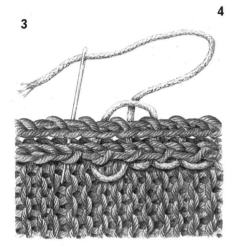

Backstitch seam (3)

This is a common method for strong seams. Place the pieces to be joined together with right sides facing, matching the rows and pattern repeats. With a tapestry needle, work in backstitch as close to the edge as possible. The stitches must be small to insure that there are no gaps left along the seam, but do not pull the seam too tightly or there will be very little "give".

Decorative raised seam (4)

This makes a neat shoulder seam. To achieve this finish, bind off on the right side of the work. Place the wrong sides of the pieces to be joined together. With a tapestry needle, pick up the outside of the bound-off stitch on one piece and take the needle across to the other bound-off edge. Work from side to side to the end of the seam.

Neat, even stitches make this decorative seam a feature of the finishing on this mercerized cotton cardigan (see page 39).

■ JOINING WITH NEEDLES

Binding off together is a method of joining two pieces of work while the stitches are still on the needles. The two pieces to be joined (most commonly at the shoulder seam) must have the same number of stitches. The finished seam forms a ridge and is visible on the right side of the garment.

Do not bind off the shoulder edge stitches, and finish knitting on a wrong side row. There should be the same number of stitches on both needles.

With the knitting needles parallel, and with the wrong sides of the work together, take a third needle and knit the first stitch on both needles together

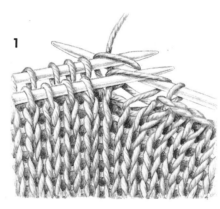

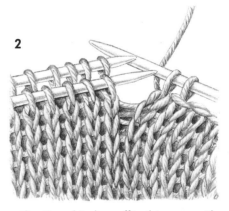

(1). Knit the second stitch on both needles together (2) and bind the first stitch off over the second.

Continue binding off in this way until only one stitch remains. Fasten off securely.

■ HEMMING

In place of ribbing, make a hem to give a flat, professional finish that won't curl up. Work an extra number of rows for the desired depth of the hem. Bind off loosely in the usual way. Turn the hem down and slipstitch the bound-off edge to the garment.

There is another method of hemming in which you do not bind off as usual but finish work on a right side row. Leave the stitches on the knitting needle. Thread a tapestry needle with the main yarn and with the wrong side facing you, take the yarn through the first stitch on the knitting needle, slip it off, then pick up a stitch on the row of the garment to which the hem is to be attached. Continue until all the stitches are sewn down.

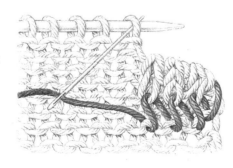

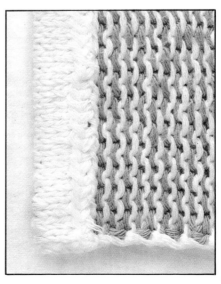

The edge of this shawl collar has been neatly hemmed (see page 47). If you hem any other edge of a garment, such as the bottom of a T-shirt without ribbing, remember that the hem will produce a bulkier fabric which may accentuate your waist or hips.

117

▪ BLOCKING AND PRESSING

Before the separate sections of the garment are sewn together, they may have to be blocked into shape so that they match the diagram measurements. This process can be carried out either by pressing with an iron and damp cloth or by dampening the pieces completely.

Place the individual pieces on a padded surface – an ironing board or a towel or blanket. Pin each piece, right side down, all along the edges so that the rows are horizontal and there is no distortion of the shape. Don't block out or press the ribbing or any other raised part of the pattern such as a cable.

For wet blocking, spray the piece with water and leave it to dry. For pressing to block, place a damp cloth over the piece of knitting and press each section evenly with a warm iron, pressing down and lifting the iron off the fabric. Do not push the iron over the work, for this may distort the fabric.

Whether you have wet the pieces for blocking or they are still damp from the steaming, leave them to dry out naturally.

▪ WASHING

The first time a cotton garment is washed, you may notice that the feel of the fabric has altered. There is a tendency for some cotton yarns to bulk up and so feel stiffer. This can also change the overall dimensions. After pressing and wearing, the fabric will relax a little, but not always back to its original gauge. For this reason, your gauge swatch should be washed and retested (see page 110). Wash cotton in lukewarm water with a mild detergent. Do not rub. Rinse several times in lukewarm water.

wring out to remove excess water. Squeeze or spin for a short time to reduce the bulk of water and consequently the weight. Lay the garment flat on a towel and reshape while it is still damp. Leave it to dry away from direct heat.

▪ FINISHING TOUCHES

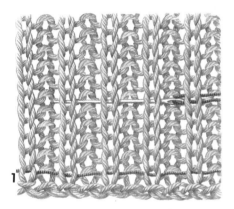

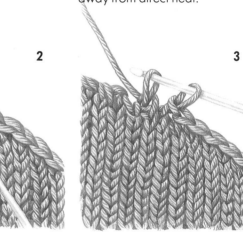

Elastic in ribbing (1)

If after the garment is finished you feel that the ribbing is not tight enough, you can thread shirring elastic under the vertical stitches on about every fourth or fifth row of the ribbing to give a tight, even fit. You can knit shirring elastic into the ribbing at the outset, see page 113.

Taping seams

If you have knitted a large garment in cotton, the weight of the yarn may distort the shape, pulling on the seams so that gradually the shoulder seams will "grow" in length. To prevent this stretching, sew a piece of seam binding along one side of the shoulder seam. Cut the binding to the length of the seam, hold it against the wrong side of one of the shoulder edges and backstitch through the binding and the two pieces of knitting. This will maintain the original length of the shoulder seam and reduce stress on the neckline.

Crochet edge

If the edges of the garment are not ribbed, as is often the case on a vest or bolero, it is advisable to finish and firm up the bottom edge with a trim to prevent it from curling. With the right side facing, using a crochet hook approximately the same size as the knitting needles (2), work one row of slip stitch or single crochet (3). Work the stitches evenly along the edge. It is important that the intervals between the stitches be consistent.

Special note: The garments in this book are designed specifically for cotton yarns, and we strongly recommend that only cotton or cotton-blend yarns be used for them. If, however, you decide to substitute another type of yarn, such as wool or acrylic, you should *disregard* the blocking instructions given with the pattern and treat the work as appropriate for the yarn used. If in doubt, check with the yarn store or with the manufacturer.

YARN MANUFACTURERS

We have chosen to show a length of the main yarn used in the patterns down the side of the first page of the pattern. Take the book to your local yarn store and check their stock against the life-size sample. Your dealer may be able to give you further information and advice about the availability of the yarns.

If you have difficulty finding the yarns you want locally, you might try contacting one of the yarn manufacturers listed below (they all carry cotton yarns).

Some companies will send sample yarn cards or lists of yarn stores on request. And some will allow you to order yarn through the mail if there are no yarn stores in your area.

Anny Blatt
24770 Crestview Court
Farmington Hills, MI 48018

Susan Bates
Rte. 9A
Chester, CT 06412

Berger du Nord
12075 N.W. 39th Street
Coral Springs, FL 33065

Bernat Yarns and Crafts
Depot and Mendon Streets
Uxbridge, MA 01569

Berroco Yarns
Elmdale Road
Uxbridge, MA 01569

Brunswick Yarn Company
Box 276
Pickens, SC 29671

Bucilla
150 Meadowlands Parkway
P.O. Box 1534
Secaucus, NJ 07094-9974

Busse Yarns
Joan Toggitt Ltd.
35 Fairfield Place
West Caldwell, NJ 07006

Caron
Avenue E and 1st Street
Rochelle, IL 61068

Coats & Clark
P.O. Box 1010
Toccoa, GA 30577

Columbia-Minerva
P.O. Box 14
High Shoals, NC 28077

Conshohocken Cotton Company
Ford Bridge Road
Conshohocken, PA 19428

Copley U.S.A. Inc.
8 Shelter Drive
Greer, SC 29651

Crystal Palace Yarns
3006 San Pablo Avenue
Berkeley, CA 94702

Di Vie U.S.A., Ltd.
P.O. Box 337
North Salem, NY 10560

The DMC Corporation
107 Trumbull Street
Elizabeth, NJ 07206

Élite
12 Perkins Street
Lowell, MA 01854

Erdal Yarns Ltd.
303 5th Avenue
New York, NY 10016

Joseph Galler Yarns
27 West 20th Street
New York, NY 10011

Lily Craft Products
140 Kero Road
Carlstadt, NJ 07072

Lion Brand Yarns
1270 Broadway
New York, NY 10011

Marnel Yarns
199 Trade Zone Drive
Ronkonkoma, NY 11779

Melrose Yarns
1305 Utica Avenue
Brooklyn, NY 11203

Merino Yarns
230 5th Avenue
New York, NY 10001

Neveda Yarns
199 Trade Zone Drive
Ronkonkoma, NY 11779

Phentex USA, Inc.
Hammon Lane
Plattsburgh, NY 12901

Phildar
6438 Dawson Boulevard
Norcross, GA 30093

Pingouin Corporation
P.O. Box 100
Highway 45
Jamestown, SC 29453

Plymouth Yarns
P.O. Box 28
Bristol, PA 19007

Reynolds Yarns
15 Oser Avenue
Hauppauge, NY 11788

Rowan Yarns
Westminster Trading
5 Northern Boulevard
Amherst, NH 03031

Schauffhauser Yarns
3489 N.W. Yeon Avenue
Portland, OR 97210

Scheepjeswool
155 Layfayette Avenue
N. White Plains, NY 10603

Spring Brook Yarns
P.O. Box 630 East Street
Ware, MA 01082

Tahki
92 Kennedy Street
Hackensack, NJ 07601

William Unger & Company, Inc.
230 5th Avenue
New York, NY 10001

Welcomme Pernelle
P.O. Box 179
Moorpark, CA 93020

ACKNOWLEDGMENTS

The publishers would like to thank the following people for their help and advice during the production of this book: Julie Dumbrell for pattern writing and checking; Ann Morgan and Sally-Anne Elliott for technical text; Jenny Bancroft for lending her collection of cotton yarn; Vivienne Studholme for knitting samples for photography; Barbara Jones (Artistic Licence) for hair and make-up; Sue Gibson and Rachael Rackow (Bookings) for the modelling; Fanny Rush for the styling for fashion photography; *Accessorize* for all jewellery and sunglasses (except on pages 62, 78, 86); Sheena Salter of the Designers' Collective for introductions to some of the designers; and Mary Tebbs for a final check on the patterns.

Editor Charyn Jones
Art Editor Louise Tucker

Managing Editor Susan Berry
Art Director Debbie MacKinnon

Fashion Photography
Sandra Lousada
Still-life photography
Chris Crofton, assistant Jayne Pearce

Charts and measurement diagrams
David Ashby
Step-by-step illustration
Sandra Pond
Fashion illustration
Sally-Anne Elliott

Reproduction F.E. Burman, London

THE DESIGNERS

Vivienne Bannister gave up school teaching to design hand- and machine- knitted garments full time. She sells her designs through retail outlets in London, New York and California and through Partyplan in the southeast of England.
Woodstock, The Avenue, Fairlight, East Sussex, U.K.

Sue Bradley is an internationally-recognized designer of exciting knitwear. Her patterns are published regularly in magazines and by the yarn companies. A book of her knitwear entitled *Stitches in Time* was published in 1986. Her designs sell in Britain, the United States and Canada.
P.O. Box 549, Bath BA1 1YA.

Joan Chatterley, a graduate of the Royal College of Art, is a busy and prolific designer with her own shop in London. She also sells her designs through retail outlets in the United States and Japan. Her work has been featured in a number of books and magazines, and she designs regularly for a major yarn manufacturer.
Unit 30b, Camden Lock, Chalk Farm Road, London NW1.

Lotte Courts is a self-taught knitter. Her interest in knitting started with her training as a painter and her talent for mixing colors. She prefers to work on private commission only.
92 Heath Street, London NW3, U.K.

Alison Ellen sells through galleries and exhibitions and on private commission. Most of her designs are knitted in one piece on circular needles, and she tries to keep the technique simple while exploring the potential of working with many colors.
Jeffreys Cottage, Dockenfield, Farnham, Surrey, U.K.

Sally-Anne Elliott, a graduate of the Royal College of Art in London, specializes in machine-knitted garments for both men and women. She also designs hand knits and socks, which she sells with her knitwear collections throughout Britain and Europe. She is a part-time lecturer at the St. Martin's School of Art in London.
669 Wandsworth Road, London SW8, U.K.

Toni Hicks and Nadine Hobro are a design partnership who got together to develop a collection of highly original shapes and structures. They have wide experience in the knitwear industry, having received commissions from home and abroad. They both teach at fashion and textile colleges in London.
3 Holdenby Road, London SE24 2DA, U.K.

Zoe Hunt has been associated with Kaffe Fassett for many years. She is now a name in her own right at the top of British knitwear design. She has had her work exhibited and sells her designs by private commission only.
c/o Frances Lincoln Ltd, Apollo Works, 5 Charlton Kings Road, London NW5 2SB, U.K.

Ann Morgan worked full time in the fashion industry for some years before deciding to sell her own range of designer knitwear. She currently works as a freelance designer for yarn companies and produces patterns for brochures as well as original designs for magazines. She also works part time as a lecturer in knitwear.

Sue Turton developed her own classic design collection after her long, successful association with Edina Ronay. She now sells throughout Britain and the United States. Her designs are regularly featured in British fashion magazines and she has recently opened a shop in Nottingham selling her own hand knits and designer clothes.
17 Lincoln Grove, Radcliffe on Trent, Nottingham, U.K.

Janice Wilkins worked as a designer for a knitting machine manufacturer after graduating from the St. Martin's School of Art. She then set up on her own and now sells both hand knits and machine knits through major retail outlets in Britain, the Continent and the United States.
10 Partridge Avenue, Larkfield, Kent ME20 6LT, U.K.